INAPPROPRIATE JOKE BOOK FOR ADULTS

INTRODUCTION

Welcome to a world of laughter and amusement!

This book is not just another compendium of jokes; it's an infectious laugh contagion waiting to spread joy like a wildfire. It contains more than 300 inappropriate jokes for adults that dare to tread where others fear to laugh. These jokes are irreverent, audacious, and are guaranteed to tickle not just your funny bone, but your entire skeleton.

From risqué puns to suggestive one-liners, we've got every flavor of humor that's fit for the comedy connoisseur with an appetite for the naughty. So, whether you're looking for a fun way to break the ice at parties, or simply a means to bring a little laughter into your day-to-day life, we've got you covered.

But remember, this book is not for the faint of heart. If you enjoy humor that's a little off the beaten path, a tad bit audacious, and a whole lot hilarious, then buckle up. You're in for one wild, comedic ride.

If these jokes brought a smile to your face, or even better, a hearty laugh, please take a moment to leave a review. Your feedback helps us continue to bring laughter into the lives of readers like you.

So dive in, and let the fun begin!

A guy finds his wife in bed with a close friend.

He takes out his gun from the closet and kills his friend. The wife says to him:
- With that attitude, you'll end up without any friends!

A man is detained by the police:

- Everything you say can and will be used against you!
- Boobs...

What did Adam say to Eve on their first date?

Move aside, I don't know how big it's going to get.

Two old men are talking in the park.

 - Women are luckier than men when they get old, says the first one.
How so? asks the second.
- Well, you see... I can barely remember what it was like to make love to my wife, and she's healthier than ever!

- What do you mean she's healthier now??
- Well, you see... When we were young, every time we got into bed, she always had migraines. Now that she's older, she hasn't had a migraine in years!

An old lady with an old man, at a nursing home,

sit on a bench every day, and the old lady holds the old man's penis in her hand each time. After a while, he sees him sitting on a bench with another old lady holding his penis:
- What does she have that I don't? the old lady asks.
- Parkinson's, the old man replies.

While having sex with my secretary in an extraordinary position, my wife walked into the office.

- You can't do this to me!
_ I know, I told her that's why I'm doing it with her!

Two lesbians are walking down the street.

At some point, a sexy girl passes by. One of the lesbians says:
- Look at those long legs the girl has!
- Uh-huh!
- And those breasts! You can even see them from behind.
- Uh-huh!
- And that appetizing ass!
- Uh-huh!
- Why are you just saying "uh-huh"? Say something else.
The other lesbian takes out a piece of paper and writes on it:
- "I can't! My tongue got hard!"

Last night I took a girl home to have sex.

After the first round, I ask her:
- One more?
- Sure, why not... she replies with a smile.
- That's when I shout: George, come on, join in!

I have to warn you, my husband will be back in 30 minutes.

- But I'm not doing anything dishonorable!
- That's exactly it... And time is passing.

Little Red Riding Hood was going to her grandmother's house

when she is caught and raped by the big bad wolf. He asks her:
- What will you tell your grandmother?
- That I met you and you raped me four times.
- Four times? the wolf is surprised.
- Yes! Or are you in a hurry?

There was a parrot, and a guy bought a box of Viagra.

He left them near the cage, and when he returned, the parrot had taken them all. To make him recover, he puts him in the freezer. After 2 hours, he opens the freezer, and the sweaty parrot says:
-Dude, it's hard to spread the legs on these chicks!

A man goes to a psychiatrist:

- Doctor, my wife is unfaithful. Every evening, she goes to the fishermen's bar and hooks up with men. Even worse, she

sleeps with anyone who asks her! I'm going crazy! What do you think I should do?
The doctor replies:
- Relax, take a deep breath, and try to calm down. Now tell me, where exactly is this bar?

At the baby bottle production machine, there was a noticeable 'fssss-pac' sound it made.

The guide explains to the visitors:
- That hissing sound is the rubber being injected, and the 'pac' is the puncture made at the tip.
The visitors then enter the condom section. There is an infernal noise here too: 'fsss-fsss-fsss-pac'.
Intrigued, the visitors ask:
- Alright, we understand why it makes the 'fsss' sound, but why do we also hear the 'pac'?
- Well, the machine works just like the one for producing baby bottles, and on the fourth condom, it pokes a hole in it.
- What the hell?! You poke holes in condoms?
- Yeees... it's good for the baby bottle business.

Little Red Riding Hood walks through the forest

and meets the wolf, who says to her:
- Little Red, you have a little frog, and I have a little key. Let's

open your little frog with my little key.
Little Red Riding Hood agrees. Later, Little Red Riding Hood arrives at her grandmother's house.
- What are you doing, Little Red?
- I'm fine, Granny. You know, I met the wolf and he told me he has a little key, and I have a little frog, and together we'll open my little frog with his little key.
- Damn that wolf. He told me he had a trumpet and made me blow it...

Father, I want to confess.

My daughter, you already confessed this morning.
Father, there has been a data update in the meantime...

In school, during the art class.

Teacher:
-Children, draw a nut!
Johnny puts his hand in his pocket...
Mary notices and immediately shouts:
-Mr. Teacher... Johnny is cheating!

Johnny and Mary, newly married.

One day, while Mary was away from home, Johnny was working in the yard.
Will appears and shouts from afar:
-Johnyyy!... Hey, Johnyyy!... Your Mary is in the cornfield with George!...

Upon hearing this, Johnny becomes furious, grabs a pitchfork, and rushes towards the field. After a while, he returns with his hat on the back of his head, happily whistling. Will asks him:
-Well, what's the matter?!?...
Johnny tactfully responds:
-Everything is fine!... It's not my cornfield!!!...

Two lovers are arguing:

-Your mustache is poking me.
-And that's a reason to break up with me?
-Yes, Mary, it is.

Two old ladies are talking on the phone:

-My husband is in the hospital! They removed his appendix!
-Really?! What's that?!?
-Something small and useless in the lower abdomen.
-Ah, I see! My husband has one of that too!

-What's the similarity between a man and a mouse?

-They both go for the hole.

Three promiscuous women and a drunkard were having sex in a street corner at 2:00 in the morning.

A police patrol passes by and takes the four of them to the station. When they arrive at the police station, they are asked for their names, first names, and occupations. The first woman says:
-Smith, Mary, bank manager.
The second woman says:
-Johnson, Jane, event organizer.
The third woman says:
-Brown, Alice, engineer.
The drunkard says:
-Oh, I must be going crazy, it turns out I'm the prostitute!

At the pharmacy:

–One condom, please.
–Just one?
–Yes. I'm trying to quit.

Two friends are talking:

–Time passes so quickly, complains one of them.
–Why do you say that?
–Well, I sleep with my wife twice and boom... another year has passed!

–How's your love life going?

–Well, I make love just like I take photos...
–What do you mean?
–Mostly selfies!

Grandpa is trying to make love to grandma.

He struggles, he tries for a long time, and finally he stops and exclaims angrily:
-Damn it, Joe Biden... and Kamala too!
-But what do they have to do with it, John?
What do you mean? Did something like this ever happen to me during Bill Clinton's time?

A woman comes home and tells her husband:

-Do you remember all the headaches I've had over the years? Well, I don't have them anymore.
-You don't have headaches anymore? the husband asks.
-What happened?
The wife replies:
-One of my friends recommended a hypnotist to me. He told me to stand in front of a mirror, stare at myself, and repeat 'I have no headache; I have no headache; I have no headache.' And it worked! The headaches disappeared.
The husband remarks:
-Well, that's amazing.
-Then the wife says:
-You know, you haven't been much of a "macho" in bed in recent years. Why don't you go to this hypnotist and see if he can help you with this problem?
The husband agrees to give it a try.
After the session, the husband comes home, tears off his clothes, picks up his wife and carries her into the bedroom. He lays her on the bed and says:

—Don't move, I'll be right back.
He goes to the bathroom, returns after a few minutes, and jumps into bed, making passionate love to his wife like he never had before.
His wife is astonished:
—Darling, that was amazing!
The man says:
—Don't move, I'll be right back.
He goes back to the bathroom, stays there for a few minutes, returns to the bedroom, and the second round is even better than the first.
The wife is left amazed and ecstatic.
The man says again:
—Don't move, I'll be right back.
And he goes to the bathroom once more.
This time, the wife quietly follows him and there, in the bathroom, she sees him standing in front of the mirror, repeating:
—She is not my wife. She is not my wife. She is not my wife...!

Two little girls were making a snowman.

First girl:
—It's ready now, it's ready!
Second girl:
—I'll quickly go inside the house to get a carrot!
First girl:
—Bring two carrots, maybe we can give it a nose too!

-What's the difference between a child and a husband?

-Almost none, except you can't leave the husband alone with the nanny!

Johnny invites Mary to a buffet.
- Mary, what drink does your heart desire?
-French champagne!
-Look at you! Vodka or beer aren't good enough? Did you only drink champagne at your dad's place?
-No, Johnny, my dad didn't want to f*ck me!

A guy is standing in line at the supermarket
when suddenly he notices a very beautiful woman also in line, a bit further back. She waves at him and smiles friendly...
The guy can't believe that such a hot woman knows him, so he asks:
-Excuse me, do we know each other?
-I'm not completely sure, but I think you're the father of one of my children, replies the beauty.
The guy remembers the only time he cheated on his wife.
-Oh my God, so you're the stripper I hooked up with the night before my wedding, on the pool table, in front of all the guys...

while your colleague whipped me with a wet celery stick on the ass?
-No, the woman replies coldly, I'm your son's English teacher.

What does audacity mean?

Audacity is when the husband comes home at midnight, smelling of perfume, with lipstick marks on his shirt, finds his wife waiting for him ready to explode, and calmly says:
-Honey, do not be upset. It's your turn!

-You scoundrel, you took my daughter's virginity!

says the mother of my friend.
-I apologize, ma'am, it won't happen again!

-Sweetheart, I had a slip-up with another man...

-Can you repeat that?
-Sure, I'm meeting him again tomorrow evening.

–How did you get the black eye???

–I was at a friend's place, making love, when we heard the front door key turning...
–It's my husband! Go through the back, said my friend...
–Now I'm thinking it would have been better if I ran, but you don't get such invitations every day!

–Claudia, I miss you!

–I'm Diana, you idiot!

–Well, I miss you too.

He:

–I swear I've fallen in love with you!
She:
–And what about your wife?
He:
–No, just me.

-Honey, are you sleeping?

-I've told you not to ask stupid questions. Shut up, put it in, get it on, and let me sleep.

-Sweetheart, who are you talking to on the phone?!

-Oh, you caught me, my love. I confess I found myself a mistress!
-Listen, don't you dare lie to me! You ordered pizza again, you damn glutton!

A guy calls a radio station to dedicate a song:

-I would like to send "Happy Birthday" to my girlfriend!
-The husband?
-Well, to her husband, I wish him good health...

A man is talking to his ex-girlfriend whom he has separated from:

-I miss you, come back home.
-I can't forgive you, you know I hate lies and yet you lied to me.
-Honey, I should be the one upset because I found you in bed with someone else.
-That's because you lied to me, saying you would come on Sunday and you came on Saturday.

A man calls the emergency room:

-Come quickly, my little boy swallowed a condom!
After a few minutes, the same man calls again:
-You don't need to come anymore, I found another one!

Late at night, the husband, drunk, comes home with his face covered in lipstick and foundation.

His wife, standing at the door, is furious.
-Honey, you won't believe it! I got into a fight with a clown!

My ex-girlfriend bent the hood of my car after we broke up.

In a way, it was my fault too because I had speed.

A blonde's husband returns home from a trip

and enters the bedroom, where he finds a naked man lying in bed. He opens the closet and finds his wife hiding there.
-How many times do I have to tell you, my dear? He should be hiding, not you!

After the surgery, the doctor tells the patient:

-I'll send my nurse to you tonight.
To which the patient responds:
-Please send her tomorrow night, I don't feel strong enough today.

A beautiful blonde goes to the gynecologist.

After placing her on the examination table with her legs open, the gynecologist starts examining her carefully, then says:
-Fantastic, faaantastic, faaantastic!
-It would have been enough for you to say "fantastic" once, no need to repeat it!
-Well, I said it once, the rest was the echo.

A guy and his wife go to the pharmacy to buy some Viagra pills.

He complains:
-What?! $10 for one pill!
To which his wife responds:
-Oh, come on, $40 a year is not that expensive...

A cowboy in the Wild West says to an Indian:

-Hey, if you make my horse laugh, I'll let you live!
The Indian whispers something to the horse's ear, and the horse bursts into laughter!
-Hey, I feel like you fooled me, but if you make my horse cry, I'll give you a thousand dollars!
-Alright, man!
He takes the horse, leads it around the corner, shows it

something, and the horse starts crying uncontrollably!
-Hey, Indian, I'll give you two thousand dollars if you tell me what's going on.
-Well, the first time I told him I had a bigger penis than him, and he laughed!
-And then?!
-And then I showed it to him!

An elderly lady of 80 comes to the pharmacy

with a prescription. The pharmacist asks her:
-Is the prescription for you?
-Yes.
-You know that it's a prescription for birth control pills? They won't do anything for you.
-Oh, yes, they make me sleep peacefully.
-How so?
-I take one pill every morning, crush it, and dissolve it in my 16-year-old granddaughter's glass of juice. That's how I sleep peacefully!

-Why are bankers good in bed?

-Because they know there's a penalty for early "withdrawal"!

Two flowers are talking in a field:

-Do you love me?

-Yes, I love you.

-Then let's call a bee!

At the market, a man is selling a rooster.

A buyer asks:
-Does it mate with hens?
-It mates with pigeons, ducks, hens, turkeys, even pigs.
-Then why are you selling it?
-Lately, it's been giving me strange looks...

Saint Peter is walking in the park one day and sees two statues.

He wonders to himself, "What if I give them two minutes of life to see what they do?" He breathes life into them and the statues run off into the bushes! The bushes start rustling.

After two minutes, a statue comes out and says:
-Saint Peter, just two more minutes...
They go on like this for about 5-6 hours, and then Saint Peter gets angry and says:
-I'll give them two more minutes and go see what they're up to!
He goes near the bushes and listens. From the bushes, he hears: "You hold the pigeon now and let me shit on him!"

A young zebra escapes from the circus and goes on a journey.

In a clearing, it meets a cow and says:
-Good day, unknown creature. Who are you and what do you do?
-I am a cow, and I provide people with milk...
The zebra continues on its way. It meets another animal:
-Good day, unknown creature. Who are you and what do you do?
-I am a sheep, and I provide people with wool, it replies.
The zebra continues on and this time meets a stallion:
-Good day, unknown creature. Who are you and what do you do?
-Hey, buddy! Hold on a second, take off your pajamas, and I'll show you who I am...

They say that a lovemaking session is equivalent to a day of work.

Hmm... It would be nice if a workday lasted only 3 minutes...

Husband, whispering after making love:

–Darling, did you enjoy it?

Sleepy wife:

–What do you mean, did I enjoy it?

–Well... "how was it"...

–Well, what was it?

–Darling, am I really fat?

–No, my love! You're as slender as a gazelle... or whatever that animal with the trunk is called...

A nun leaves the monastery and wanders the streets.

At some point, she meets a woman and asks:
-Hey, but what do you do to have such a beautiful car?
Nothing. I meet a German guy, make him feel good, and he gives me cars.
-And those nice clothes, where do you get them?
-I meet an Italian guy, make him feel good, and he gives me clothes.
-But where do you get all that money?
-I meet a French guy, make him feel good, and he gives me money.
The nun returns disappointed to the monastery and goes to bed.

Around midnight, there's a light knocking on the door. The nun responds:

-Go away, Father Thomas, with your biscuits and all.

The synagogue cashier had run out of money to help the poor.

Not a single penny had been deposited in the charity box for a long time. The next morning, he put a notice on the synagogue door:
-A married woman in the neighborhood is involved with an unmarried man. If by tomorrow morning there is no $100 bill in the charity box, I will have to reveal their names.
The next day, he found 30 $100 bills and one $50 bill in the charity box, with a note attached: "Wait until tomorrow, I need to gather the money!"

What do women have once a month that lasts for 3-4 days?

Their husband's salary.

An alien and a muscular guy on a bus:

-Piu piu! and the alien pushes the guy with its finger.
-Hey, stop it, or I'll beat you up!
-Piu piu! and it pushes him again.
-Stop it, or I'll cut off your organ!
-But I don't have...
-Well, how do you have sex?
-Piu piu!...

Two men meet at the train station:

-What are you doing here?
-I'm looking for my wife, I lost her!
-Hey, what a coincidence, I lost mine too!
-So, what does yours look like?
-She's tall, red-haired, big breasts, and long legs!

-By the way, what does yours look like?
-Forget about mine! Let's go find yours!

John comes home from town and says to Mary, determined:

-Mary, turn off the lights, close the curtains, and get in bed quickly!
-But John, I still have work to do.

-When I say it, I mean it!
Mary sees that she has no choice but to comply. John gets into bed, pulls the blanket over them, and says:
-Now, Mary, let me show you the glow-in-the-dark watch I bought.

One evening, a police officer catches a naked man on the street.

-What are you doing naked on the street?
The panicked man replies:
-I'm a parachutist!
-Well, where is your parachute?
-Upstairs, on the second floor, her husband is beating it...

-What happened to your eye?

-My wife hit me...
-Why?
-I used the informal "you" when talking to her.
-Pfff, but what kind of relationship do you have that she would hit you for that?
-Well, last night while we were eating, she said to me, "You know, we haven't made love in 3 months."
To which I replied:
-Maybe you...

Two neighbors meet in the stairwell.

-What's wrong with you, dear? Are you sick?
-No, why do you ask?
-I saw the doctor coming out of your apartment this morning.
-So what? When three soldiers came out of your apartment, did I ask you if a war had broken out?

Priest:

-There will come a day when you will pay for all your sins!
-Nonsense, Father, I'm already paying! Women and alcohol aren't free, you know...

Between two friends:

-What's wrong, man? Why are you so upset?

-How can I not be upset! Yesterday, I came home early from work and found my wife in bed with a Chinese guy!
-Oh no! And what did you say?
-Well, what the hell could I say, I don't know Chinese...

The bear was slowly walking through the forest

when it spotted Mrs. Fox. It quickly jumps into the nearest bush and says:
-Cock-a-doodle-doo!
The fox jumps into the bush... right into the arms of the bear, who affectionately mumbles:
-Ah, my dear, I've been waiting for you!
After four rounds of "love," he releases the redhead and happily rubs his paws, saying:
-It's so good to know a foreign language!

It's 11 PM. The 24-hour pharmacy.

A guy enters, asks for a condom. Pays, leaves. The next evening, close to midnight, the same guy:
-Please give me a condom.
He takes it, pays, leaves. The following evening, the same scene. The curious pharmacist asks the guy:
-Don't mind me asking, but why do you buy them one at a time? Why don't you buy more at once?

To which the guy responds:
-You know, I actually want to quit...

A gentleman and a lady meet at a nudist beach...

The gentleman: I'm glad I met you!

The lady: I can see!

In a pharmacy, a confident young man enters,

showing the pharmacist his right hand raised with fingers spread out.

-Five, he says.
-Five what? asks the pharmacist.
-Five Viagra pills because a woman is coming over tonight, and I want to be in top form. The next day, the young man appears at the door, looking a bit down, and raises both hands in the air. The pharmacist says:
-Ten Viagra pills?
-No, hand cream because the woman didn't come...

A man goes to the doctor and confesses that he has potency problems.

The doctor says:
-That's not a problem anymore these days! A new medication called Viagra has just been released on the market, which solves all these kinds of problems.
The doctor prescribes the pill, and the man leaves. After a few months, the doctor meets the patient on the street:
-Mr. Doctor, your medication is a miracle! Thank you so much! It's amazing!
-I'm glad to hear that, says the doctor. What does your wife think about it?
-Wife?! the man asks in surprise. Well, since then, I haven't been home...

I just paid $15 for an 18-year-old girl to rub her breasts on me for 30 minutes.

Can't wait to go to the barber again!

Last night, I brought a hot chick to my place.

-Baby... you're hot! I told her.
-Go to hell! she said, "You'd be hot too if you were tied to the radiator with handcuffs!"

Two neighbors are talking:

-You know, I have some bad news for you... Your daughter got really drunk at the club last night! My son told me...
-You're lying, she didn't put anything in her mouth last night!
-Hmm, I have to tell you, she lied to you about that too...

Finally, at the New Year's Eve party, I met an honest woman.

She told me straight away:
-If you want to sleep with me, you'll have to be patient.
-There were three men ahead of me...

A man wants to buy thong underwear for his wife.

The saleswoman asks:
-What size would you like?
-Hmm, hard to say...
-It's important to know the size...
-I know... size 77!
-77?! That size doesn't exist! How did you come up with that size?
-Well, we have a 32-inch TV at home, and when she stands in front of it, there are about two centimeters of space left on each side!

A lovely young lady is hitchhiking by the side of the road.

A truck passes by, stops, and picks her up. Before getting comfortable, she takes off her panties and puts them in her backpack.

-What are you doing, woman? the shocked driver asks.
-I know truck drivers! I take them off because you'll get engine oil all over them...

For my wife's birthday, I bought her a boxer.

Despite having a flattened nose, bulging eyes, and those waves of fat hanging, the dog seems to like her...

A woman sued the hospital, claiming that after a recent treatment, her husband lost interest in sex.

The hospital spokesperson stated:
-We don't understand the reasons for the complaint, ma'am. All we did was correct her husband's vision!

A guy had to leave the country for a month,

so he asked his best friend to keep an eye on his wife and let him know if anything special happens.

After 2 weeks, he receives a telegram:
"The man who used to come to your wife every night was absent yesterday!"

Last night, I saw a nice girl at the bar,

approached her, and asked if I could buy her a drink.
-Don't you have a girlfriend? she asked. Guys like you always have a girlfriend... No, unfortunately, we broke up a month ago, I assure her.
-Oh, I'm sorry, she sighed... Come, let's have a glass of wine together, my treat.
After a few drinks, a kiss, and an embrace, we woke up in her bed at her place, and we made love like crazy.
While I was getting dressed, getting ready to leave, the girl said to me:
-So... You look great, you're a good guy, and on top of that, you're amazing in bed! Can I ask how on earth you broke up with your girlfriend?
-My wife found out! I replied hastily...

-Oh, your husband has a big nose!

-Yes, the woman blushes, but it's not true.

In a bus, on the same seat, a man and a woman with a baby were sitting. At one point, the woman takes out her breast to breastfeed the baby. The baby turns its nose to the side and refuses to suckle. The woman, upset, tells him:
–Eat, or I'll give it to that man!
They arrive in Washington, the same scene repeats: the woman takes out her breast to breastfeed the baby. The baby turns its nose to the side and refuses to suckle. The woman, once again upset, tells him:
–Eat, or I'll give it to that man!
The baby remains uninterested. They arrive in Baltimore, the scene repeats itself, and the baby still refuses. The woman repeats her line:
– Eat, or I'll give it to that man!
The bus continues on its way. The man sitting next to the woman on the seat finally bursts out:
–Make up your mind, lady, because I was supposed to get off in Washington!

Two ladies are playing golf

and having a great time until one of them hits the ball right in the middle of a group of men. Unfortunately, one of them falls to the ground, writhing in pain, with both hands between his legs. The woman rushes to him, apologizes profusely, and offers to help him because she happens to be a doctor.

-No, thanks, I'll recover in a few minutes, the man whispers, still with his hands between his legs.
Feeling terribly guilty, the young woman gently moves his hands aside, carefully unzips his pants, and starts massaging him.
-Do you feel better now? she asks at one point.
-Yes, much better, the guy groans. But my fingers still hurt!

Once, I was in bed with my wife, and I was wondering,

you know, "did she have one or not?"
Finally, I decided to ask out loud, not just in my thoughts, but in a roundabout way, and I said:
-Hey, how come I never know when you have an orgasm?
-Well, there's no point in calling you at work and bothering you for such a small thing.

A woman is having sex with a student:

-Did you finish?
-No, I'm in my fourth year!

-Darling, do you remember Sharon Stone in "Basic Instinct,"

when she crosses her legs in the police station?
-Of course, I do.
-Idiot, you remember that, but you forgot that we need to buy bread for the house, right?

A guy comes into a bar and orders a beer.

When the bartender sees him, he starts laughing hysterically.
-What are you laughing at, man? he asks.
-Dude, you're the ugliest person I've ever seen in my life. You're horribly ugly. I think it's impossible for you to get any woman.
-I wouldn't be so sure. I bet I can hook up with any woman in this bar of your choice.
-Alright, old man. Here's the bet. Look, I bet you can't even get a word with that blonde with big tits who's sitting at the table with her 6'6" boyfriend.
-Okay.
The guy goes, sits at the table with the blonde and her boyfriend, and 5 minutes later, he leaves the bar with the blonde. The bartender is completely stunned. He goes to the table, sits next to the 6'6" guy, and says:
-Dude, what the hell just happened? I don't understand anything. What did he say, what did he do?

–I don't know, man. He didn't say anything, he was just there, licking his eyebrows.

Two friends were talking in a bar:

–How's married life?
–It's great, I feel like I'm 16 again.
–What do you mean?
–I smoke in the bathroom and drink secretly.

John comes home and finds Mary undressed.

–Why are you undressed, Mary?
–Well, I don't have anything to wear!...
–What do you mean, you don't? asks John and opens the wardrobe.
–Look: skirts, blouses, pants... Hello, George!... dresses...

In a train compartment with two intellectuals,

there was also a peasant named George who was witnessing their conversation:
-Where do you send your wife to relax?
-To the seaside, where she comes back cheerful, tanned, and I don't have any trouble with her for a year.
-And you?
-To the mountains, fresh air, greenery, she comes back relaxed, rejuvenated, I don't have any trouble with her for a year.
The two intellectuals nudge each other and ask George:
-And you, sir, where do you send your wife to relax?
-Well, my dears, I f**k her myself!

Johnny and George are having a conversation:

-Johnny! How about we get two girls, go to the sauna, drink champagne, and make love?
-Well, how about, in front of the girls???

Buddy George goes to a Sex Shop.

-Give me a second-hand inflatable doll!
-But why do you want a used one, buddy?
-Because I like the experienced ones!

Johnny and George, retired, have a chat:

–My wife has gone crazy...
–Really, what happened?
–Lately, she wants to suck my pajamas...
–Oh, come on... how's that possible?
–Last night I was peacefully watching a match, and she comes and tells me to take off –my pajamas...
Why, I ask her?!
–So she can suck it, she says!

Buddy George comes down from the mountains

to the city after a year of work. Extremely happy, he enters a restaurant, eats well, drinks well, smokes a cigarette...
The waiter asks him:
–Can I get you anything else, buddy?
–Well, I've eaten, I've drunk, I've smoked a cigar... well, if only there were a girl now...!
–Buddy, we don't have any girls... but if you want Willy, that's an option...
–No, man, I'm not into that...
–Buddy George leaves and comes back after a year, same story, same response: no, man, I'm not into that.
The next year, the same thing...
After another year, George gathers his courage and says:

-Well, I'll try with Willy, but I prefer privacy...
-It's not possible... there are five of us...

-Five? asks George.
-Yeah, me, you, Willy, and two guys holding Willy, because he's not into that either...

Buddy George goes to the doctor.

The doctor asks him:
-Do you smoke?
George thinks for a moment and answers, gesturing with his hand left and right:
-So-so...
What do you mean "so-so"? Approximately how much?
-Well, what can I say? Around 4 packs a day.
-Do you have sex?
-So-so. Around 5 times a day.
-I see. And do you drink?
-Oh, yes! I drink!

-Hey, George, what's up with your bull, the one that had no strength?

-He's doing well, the vet gave him tablets, and now he's doing his job.

-And what are those tablets called?
-I don't know, man, what they're called, but they have a minty taste.

Buddy George at the doctor's:

-Good day, Miss Doctor...
-How can I help you, sir?
-I don't know how to tell you... I can't have sex.
-It can be resolved, don't worry. Here's a prescription, you take the medication every evening, and come back in a week to see how it went.
Buddy George returns after a week, twirling his hat in his hand... the doctor asks him directly:
-Is there any improvement, buddy?
-Nothing...
-I prescribed you the strongest medications, it should have worked... here's what we'll do! I'll lie down on the bed, undress, and you try to see what you feel!
Buddy George gets heated, quickly gets down to business, and has intercourse with the doctor like there's no tomorrow.
-See, buddy, you can do.
- Here, of course I can, but at home I don't have anybody to do it with.

Farmer George comes home unexpectedly

and finds his wife giving oral pleasure to their neighbor, Johnny.

-That's it, Mary! Bite it hard, because otherwise, he's going to want to f*ck you!!!

Johnny and George go on separate vacations.

Johnny returns from his winter vacation satisfied.
-Well, where have you been, Johnny?
-In Sweden!
And how are the Scandinavians?
Johnny avoids giving a clear answer. Back home, he searches in the dictionary.
"Aha, Scandinavians, meaning the women there! How did I not know, I could have bragged, I had the chance!"
The following year, Johnny returns tanned from his vacation.
-Well, Johnny, where else have you been?
-Egypt, beautiful country!
-And how was Egypt, Johnny?
-Beautiful, hot, camels, sand, sun...
-And the pyramids?
-A bunch of whores....

Two blondes at the cinema, one whispers to the other:

-The guy next to me is masturbating!
-It's okay, just ignore him.
-I can't, he's using my hand!

Two blondes talking:

-Hey, girl, last night I slept with Mary's husband!
-Oh, really?! Well, how was it?
-He's actually great in bed, I don't know what she's complaining about!
-See, when I told you that Mary's husband is better than yours in bed, you didn't believe me!!!

Today, sperm cells held a moment of silence

For their fallen comrades in '69!

The basic rule for winter sex:

If your nose isn't running, you should be on top!

-Kids, let's see how imaginative you are.

Look, I'm going to wave a white handkerchief. What does it suggest to you...
Johnson:
-Well, teacher, I imagine a train. My mom is leaving, I'm standing on the platform waving a white handkerchief.
-Good. And you, student Smith?
-I'm crying because my sister is taken to the hospital, and from the window, I wave a white handkerchief.
-Very good. And you, Johnny?
-I'm thinking about p*ssy.
-Shame on you, you jerk. Get out. How can you think about such a thing when I'm waving a white handkerchief.
-Well, you'll see, teacher, you can wave a boat at me, but I still think about p*ssy!

Tarzan and Jane are having sex.

-Tarzan, my dear, there's the belly button, the hole... it's lower!

-Tarzan is strong, he makes a hole wherever he wants!

Mary and George - their first night together.

-George, I'm cold!
-Take the whole blanket!
After a while, Mary tries again:
-George, I'm still cold! Can't you warm me up?
-Of course, Marie, I'll get you an extra comforter!
Again, after some time, Mary says:
-George, I'm still not warm... can't you warm me up?
-Come on, I'll get you the duvet too!
Seeing that George doesn't understand what she wants, Mary decides to be more direct:
-George, don't you realize that I have a hole too?
-Well, you're stupid, aren't you? The cold comes in through there!!!!

John and Mary are making love.

At one point, Mary exclaims:
-John, I'm having an orgasm... Oh... Oh!
John angrily gets out of their conjugal bed and replies:
-Listen, Mary, no one comes while I'm f*cking you, got it?

In a village, a young and beautiful teacher arrives.

A handsome young man is sent to greet her.
He politely puts her luggage in the cart and sits in front, next to the young lady.
At the edge of the village, they see a cow mating with a bull. Being from the city, the teacher is deeply affected and asks the young man:
-How does the bull know... you know... when it's the right time?
-By the smell of the cow...
They continue walking and see a horse and a mare doing the same thing.
-And how does the horse know...? the curious teacher asks again.
-Also by the smell, the same goes for dogs and sheep.
They reach the new residence of the teacher, unload the luggage, and the young man bids her farewell:
-All the best!
-Thank you for your help, says the young teacher. Drop by sometime when your nose gets clean...

Deaf-mutes can be excellent gynecologists.

There's no need to listen to anything, everything is read on the lips!

Little Johnny enters his parents' room

and sees his mom with her skirt lifted and his dad behind her. Upon seeing him, the father laughs and signals for him to leave and close the door. After finishing, the father goes to see what the son is doing... and finds him in the room with his grandma, who also had her skirt lifted, and little Johnny was behind her... at which point the father yells:
-Johnny, what the hell are you doing there?
-It's not so funny when it's about your mom, is it?

On a bench, a mother is breastfeeding.

Next to her is a guy who is watching. After a while, he asks:
-Can I have a taste too?
-Oh, you rude person, how could you think of such a thing?
-I'll give you 100 dollars if you let me.
The woman thinks about what she has to lose and agrees.
After he sucks well, the woman gets aroused and asks subtly:
-Hey, don't you want anything else?
-Well, some bread would be nice, don't you have any?

Two friends are talking at the office...

-I don't know what to do anymore, I have a terrible neck pain.
-Ah, no problem, I recommend you a sure remedy. Every time I have a sore neck, I give my husband oral sex, and the next day I'm fine.
-Seriously?
-Yes. The next day, at the office... the sick friend appears very cheerful...
-Well, how are you feeling?
-Extraordinary... you were right, the remedy you recommended works perfectly... although your husband couldn't believe it was your idea.

A middle-aged man, well past his prime, enters a newly opened brothel.

Casting discreet glances left and right, he heads towards a table that serves as a reception desk, where a young man is busy typing on a computer.
- Hm Hm, says our man.
Oh, welcome to our computerized establishment, where services are organized according to the latest economic models, says the young man. I'm sure you want to have a pleasant time. Please proceed down this discreetly lit corridor, and if you want blondes, turn right; if you want something else, turn left.
- Hm, Hm, yes, alright, the pleasure-seeking man says and steps into the corridor on the right. In front of him, a small touch-screen selection system appears in front of two identical doors. "Do you want a) tall blonde, press 1 or b) short blonde, press 2," says the screen. Mumbling something

unintelligible, the man quickly presses 1. The door on the left immediately slides into the wall, invitingly.
Stepping inside, our increasingly "hot" client finds a discreet hallway with another touch-screen. "Do you want a tall blonde with a) big breasts, please press 1, or b) small breasts, please press 2," says the screen. Grumbling a bit louder, our man impatiently presses 1. Immediately, a door disguised in the wall opens, inviting him further.
Another corridor, adorned with beautiful nude paintings on the walls, and the familiar touch-screen: "Do you want tall blondes with big breasts and specializing in a) perversions, please press 1, or b) specializing in classic sex, please press 2," says the screen this time. Unable to control a nervous grimace, our man punches the screen roughly in the area where it says 1, and slowly, with lascivious music playing, a new door opens in front of him. He rushes through the door like a hurricane. When he looks around, he finds himself on the sidewalk outside the building. Fuming with anger, he storms around the building and re-enters the reception desk.
- What the hell is this, huh? he yells at the young receptionist.
- Well, the receptionist replies, the girls haven't arrived yet, but we hope you enjoyed our organization very much.

Two women are walking on the street late at night.

A patrol of police officers stops them. The patrol leader says:
-Good evening, I need to check your documents, please!
One of the women responds:
-I'm a flight attendant, I just arrived from a trip and I'm rushing home to take a shower and change because I've just been notified that I have to leave immediately on another trip. As I was in a hurry when I left, I forgot my bag with my work

documents. Please understand the situation, but time is pressing and I'm in a hurry.
-Alright, I understand, the police officer replies. But what about you? he asks, addressing the other woman.
Blushing, she responds:
-Well, I'm also a whore, but I don't know how to express myself.

A gipsy man goes to the priest:

-Father, I have sinned!!!
The priest puts him in confession.
-What have you sinned? Have you stolen?
-No.
-Have you raped?
-No.
-Have you killed?
-No.
-Then, what?
-I fucked a mare.
Curious, the priest asks:
-How did you manage that, considering that a mare kicks and throws you off, etc.?
-Well, Father, I dug a big hole, put the mare in the hole, and...
But the teacher from the altar interrupts:
-Listen, Father, and here we are trying with a ladder.

The son, who has just arrived on vacation from college, tells his father:

-Dad, I think... my roommate is gay.
-What makes you think that?
-Well, when I kiss him, he closes his eyes.

A truck driver picks up a young hitchhiker.

At the first stop, he stops the truck and suggests they have a quick session of sex in the grass. Said and done. After going through several positions, the young woman says:
-Don't you want to give it to me in the back?
He replies:
-Are you crazy? I have barrels and crates up there!

A promiscuous woman presents herself to the gynecologist

for a consultation. She enters the doctor's office and says:
-My dear doctor, my prune hurts, and I pee in four different directions. Is this a disease?
The gynecologist asks her to lie down, examines her, and finally says:
-I will tell you three important things: firstly, I'm not your dear doctor, secondly, what you have between your legs is not a

prune, but a watermelon, and thirdly, someone left a button in there.

A military unit is stationed in the middle of the desert,

in an oasis. The unit's commander, while looking through binoculars at what is happening in the area, notices a soldier having sex with an ostrich. The commander loses his temper and calls the soldier to him:
–I caught you doing it with an ostrich! You've brought disgrace upon the entire unit.
The soldier stands at attention and tells his commander:
–I apologize, General. I'm willing to fix my mistake. I'll take her as my wife.

A distinguished gentleman goes to the doctor.

– Please help me, doctor. My marriage is at stake. Sex is not working as it used to.
–I will prescribe a pill for you to take during dinner every evening.
After a few days, the patient goes for another medical examination for the doctor to see if the prescribed pill has any side effects.
–So, did the pill help?

-Doctor, it's truly amazing. Even during dinner, my wife and I had sex twice.
- And how about her?
- She loved it. But the guests were very surprised.

Two friends, one white and one black, were fishing by the water,

and they let their penises hang in the water.
-Wow, the water is so cold, the white guy says.
-And the bottom is so sandy, adds the black guy.

A very famous magician meets a big fan in a public restroom.

The young fan asks the magician to show him a trick; so the magician asks the fan to pull down his pants and asks him:
-Can you feel my finger in your ass?
-Yes! the fan responds.
-Look... no hands!! the magician adds.

An old man boasts to his friend at the club.

-Last night, I took three dancers home.
-Oh, superficial as I've always known you!
-And I slept with each of them.
-Oh, with your exaggerated sexual appetite!
-And I made each of them orgasm.
-Oh, you have good linguistic skills!

There was an old lady at the tram stop

who couldn't see very well, so she asked a young girl which number the incoming tram had. The young girl tells her it's number 13. To which the old lady says:
-Oh, never mind, I know what these people write, because a couple of days ago, I passed by a fence and it said "D*ck" and when I went in, it turned out to be a lumberyard.

Young Smith falls head over heels in love with a beautiful girl.

He persistently pursues her until, eventually, she agrees to go with him, there being no apartment available, in a taxi. They start heading out of town. The young man embraces the woman and whispers to the driver:
-Drive slowly, driver!

To which the taxi driver says:
-I know, I usually take Miss for a ride.

Johny goes off to the army.

His girlfriend wants a picture of him. He only has a nude photo from the beach. He cuts off the most important part and gives it to his girlfriend. His grandmother also wants a photo. Johny thinks for a moment and gives her the rest of the picture. The grandmother says:
-Look, here he is, without a nose and with a crooked tie!

Math class: The teacher says,

-Tomorrow we'll have a pop quiz!
-No absences allowed!
A student asks:
-If we're exhausted from sex, can we skip?
-You can write with the other hand!

A woman rushes into the dentist's office.

She undresses and sits on the chair with her legs apart. The shocked dentist says:
-Ma'am, I'm sorry, but the gynecologist's office is across the street!
-Shut up! You were the one who put a denture on my husband, so you're the one who will get it out.

Reportage in Afghanistan.

The reporter and an old man.
R: Tell me, sir, a happier event in your life.
M: Young man, one day, a neighbor of ours lost his goat in the mountains. We all searched for it, one day, 2, 3, and we found it. We all f*cked it.
R: Hmm, very interesting. Another adventure?
M: One day, a neighbor lost his wife in the mountains. We all searched for her, one day, 2, 3, and we found her. We all f*cked her.
R: Alright then. How about a less happy one?
M: Well... I got lost in the mountains...

A guy and a girl would come up with new ways to have sex every evening.

One evening, the man had an idea:
-Let's f*ck in your ear!
-What if I go deaf?
-Well, after last night you didn't get mute, didn't you?

A mother is teaching her daughter:

-I don't mind, you can go to your room with your boyfriend as long as we're watching TV in the living room. But if he does something he shouldn't, let us know.
-But, mom, how?
-Pay close attention... If he wants to kiss you, shout "pears." If he wants to touch your breasts, shout "apples." If he puts his hands lower, then shout "peaches"!
The young couple locks themselves in the girl's room, and the parents are watching TV. Suddenly, a voice is heard shouting:
-Fruit salad...! Fruit salad.

In the restroom of a restaurant, screams, curses, and strange noises can be heard.

The waiters, thinking that a fight is happening, enter that particular stall. Inside, a guy is holding his penis in his hand and yelling at it:
-Last night, you didn't want to get up, and now you won't let me pee?!

-Is it true that these potency pills should be swallowed as quickly as possible?

-Yes, otherwise you'll get a stiff neck.

A blind man passes by a fish market, takes off his hat, and says:

-Good day, ladies!

A salesman rang the doorbell, and little Johnny answered.

Salesman: "Is your father home?"
Johnny: "Yes."
Salesman: "Can I see him?"
Johnny: "No, he's in the shower."
Salesman: "But is your mother home?"
Johnny: "Yep."
Salesman: "Then can I see her?"
Johnny: "Nope, she's in the shower too."
Salesman: "Do you think they'll be out soon?"
Johnny: "No."
Salesman: "Why do you think that?"
Johnny: "Well, when my dad asked me to give him some lubricant, I gave him superglue."

A man was walking through the desert, thirsty and hungry,

when he saw a fancy villa with three floors, a fountain, a swimming pool, and more. In the yard, there was a man and a woman staring at each other.
- Good people, I'm thirsty. I haven't had a drink in four days. Can I drink from your fountain?
They didn't respond, just continued staring at each other. The man went, drank, and returned.
- Good people, I've been walking through the desert for who knows how long. Can I eat something from your place?
Still no response. The man ate, went back to the yard, and they were still motionless. Seeing that anything goes, the man said:

- Well... can I take your wife, just for a little bit, to the bedroom?
Again, no response. The man went, spent two hours with the woman, and continued his journey. He overheard a conversation in the kitchen:
Husband: "You whore! Shameless! How could you cheat on me right in front of my eyes, in my own house?"
To which the wife replied: "Oh! You spoke first! You're taking out the trash!"

-Well, well! the teacher says to Johnny.

Is sex the only thing you think about...? You can't make a living out of that!
-How can you say that, sir! Have you seen my older sister...!

Mary to John:

-John, let's do "something" like all the other people!
-Alright, you! When I shout once, you go to the bedroom, when I shout twice, you undress, and when I shout three times, you get in bed.
-Alright, John.
One day, John goes under Mary's window and shouts:
-Mary! Mary! Mary! You come outside! The barn is burning and you think about f*cking.

Johnny buys a new pair of boots,

and in the morning, as he wakes up, he goes and puts them on while completely naked. His wife Mary asks:
-Why is that thing hanging there?
-It's looking at my new boots, Johnny replies.
-Couldn't you also buy a new hat?!

A guy goes to a brothel and asks for the hottest prostitute in the house.

-It's $3,000, he is told.
He pays and goes to the room.
Inside, there's a stunning woman. The guy undresses and starts masturbating, to which the woman asks:
-Have you lost your mind? What are you doing?
-You, just be quiet! I'm the one having fun with my own money!

-Mary, would you scream if I pulled your panties down and had sex with you right now?

-Oh, I've never done anything like that!
-Haven't you had sex before?
-No, I've never screamed.

For years, Smith has had the bad habit of leaning his hand on the wall when he wants to get out of bed.

Over time, an ugly stain has formed on the wall, ruining the look of the bedroom.
The time comes for painting. Smith's wife guides the painter, an older man, through all the rooms of the apartment. Finally, he says:
-Please come to the bedroom, I want to show you where my husband puts his hand every morning when he wakes up.
Scared, the painter says:
-Thank you very much... But if possible, I'd rather have a shot of brandy.

A bodybuilder goes to a brothel.

When he's in the room with a lady, he starts undressing. He takes off his shirt, and the lady exclaims:

-Wow, what big biceps!
Guy: - Dynamite.
He takes off his pants.
L: - Wow, what big calves you have!
G: - Dynamite.
He takes off his tank top.
L: - Wow, what pecs!
G: - Dynamite.
Then he takes off his underwear.
L: - Wow, such a small fuse for so much dynamite.

Apparently, Johnny had a severe pain in his elbow.

He goes to the doctor, gets a bunch of tests done, but nothing is found. He hears about a clinic where they do tests on a very advanced computer. He goes there, and they give him a one-liter bottle that he needs to fill with urine. Unable to do it on his own, he's helped by his wife and daughter.
Here are the results:
-Just so you know, your wife is sleeping with the plumber, your daughter hasn't been a virgin for a long time, and you no longer masturbate in the bathroom because it's too tight, and you hit your elbow.

A banana and a vibrator are sitting on a nightstand.
The banana asks the vibrator:

–Is it your first time?
–No, why? the vibrator says.
–Well, you're shaking a lot.

A guy and a girl are in bed, going at it.

Suddenly, they hear a car screeching outside the house. The guy jumps out of bed, grabs his clothes, the girl opens the window, and the guy jumps out. After a while, there's a knock on the door. The girl opens it, and there's the guy with his clothes in his arms:
–Honey, we're so stressed!

Classmates are having a party in an apartment.

The mom, staying in another room so as not to disturb them, suddenly hears some strange sounds and enters the room in question.
–What are you all doing here, kids? she yells.
–Group sex...
–That's okay, I thought you were smoking.

A guy tattoos his girlfriend's name, "Wendy," on his penis.

The problem is that when he's not erect, you can only see the letters W and Y. One day, our guy goes to a nudist beach and sees another guy with the tattoo "Wy" on his penis, so he asks:
-Does yours say Wendy too?"
-No, mine says, "Welcome to Miami Beach. Have a nice holiday."

A gang of thieves stops a bus.

The gang leader gives orders to his men:
- Rob the men, and rape the women!
A more compassionate bandit says:
-Boss, let's leave the women alone at least!
Then a woman's voice is heard:
-Don't you meddle in your boss's affairs!

Johnson arrives home earlier

and finds his wife in bed with George, his friend. He shouts angrily:
-Is this your gratitude, you ungrateful woman? I've always pampered you, bought you everything you wanted. Is this how you repay me for the expensive fur coats, the vacations

in California...? And you, you George, at least stop it as long as I'm talking!

A worried man goes to the doctor.

- What happened? the doctor asks.
- Well, Doc, one of my testicles turned blue.
The doctor undresses him, examines him, and then says:
- Sir, I'm sorry, but it needs to be removed.
- What about me?
- Oh, don't worry, you can manage with just one.
The doctor performs the surgery, the man is fine, satisfied, but after a month he comes back to the doctor.
- Doc, the other testicle has turned blue too.
- The doctor examines him and determines that this one needs to be removed as well.
- What about me?
- It's okay, you can live without it.
The doctor operates on him, puts a bag in place, and the man is satisfied. But after a while, he comes back to the doctor.
- Doctor, my penis has turned blue.
- Oh, it's very serious, it needs to be operated on immediately.
The doctor performs the surgery, and he inserts a tube. The man manages for a while, but then he comes back to the doctor again.
- Doctor, I'm desperate, the tube has turned blue.
The man undresses, the doctor examines him, and then says, confused:
- Ahh... it's because of your jeans.

A nun gets into a taxi.

The taxi driver keeps looking at her, biting his lips.
-What's the matter, my son? asks the nun.
-Well, I'm ashamed to tell you, but I've had one sexual fantasy in my life: to receive oral sex from a nun.
-Well, my son, let's see what we can do. Just remember, you have to be Christian and unmarried.
-I am, I am, says the taxi driver, ready for a "little something."
He pulls over, and the nun does her thing, and they continue on their way. But on the road, the taxi driver starts crying.
-Forgive me, sister, I have sinned! I'm Jewish and married!
-It's alright, darling, I'm not a nun either... My name is John, and I'm going to a masquerade ball...

In the summer, at the beach, a guy enters the water.

At one point, while he's swimming freely, he feels a hand on his testicles and hears a voice from the depths:
"- Plus 2 or minus 2?"
He thinks to himself... "Better than nothing, I'll go with 4," and he says: "- Plus 2!"
When he gets out of the water, he realizes he has 4 testicles. He evaluates the situation and decides: "I'll go back in the water again, and when I feel the hand on my testicles and it asks the question, I'll say 'minus 2' and solve it!"
He goes back into the water, feels the hand on his testicles, and hears the voice from the depths: "Plus 4 or minus 4!!!!"...

A man and a woman were making love

when they hear the door open, it's the woman's husband. The man jumps out of the window naked, even though it's pouring rain outside. At that moment, a group of marathon runners passes by, and he joins the group. One of the runners asks:
-Do you always run naked?
-Yes.
-And do you always wear a condom?
-Oh, no, only when it's raining...

On the wall of a company, there was a large poster

that said they offer a treatment that guarantees a weight loss of 20 kg per week. A 100 kg overweight man comes, pays $1000, and is assigned to room 3.
He enters and sees a gorgeous blonde girl, completely naked, with a sign that says, "If you catch me, you can have me!"
The man runs after her for a week, catches her, and has sex with her. He loses about 20 kg and is very satisfied.
He comes back for the second week and requests another room. The man thinks to himself, "If it's a brunette, I'm in luck!"
He is assigned to room 4.
He enters and sees a completely naked big man with a sign that says, "If I catch you, I'll f*ck you!"

An elderly man of about 90 years old goes to get his tests done.

At the end, he asks the doctor to test his sperm. The doctor says it's not necessary, but he insists, and the doctor gives him a small container.
The next day, the old man and his wife come back, both exhausted. He tells the doctor:
-Mr. Doctor, I tried with my left hand, with my right hand, my wife tried with both hands, with her mouth, we placed it between her legs and pulled on it... How do you open this damn container?

One day, a man comes home from work. He enters the house and tells his wife:

-Undress!
The wife undresses.
-Go in front of the mirror!
The wife goes in front of the mirror.
-Stand on your head!
The wife stands on her head.
-Spread your legs!
The wife spreads her legs...
The man puts his chin between the woman's legs and says happily:

–I look good with a beak…

Husband: Why do you still wear that bra? You don't have anything to put in it!

Wife: Well, you wear underwear, don't you?!

A man looks satisfied in front of a mirror at his manhood:

–If it were just five centimeters longer, I would be the king!

His wife looks disappointed at him and says:

–If it were just five centimeters shorter, you would be the queen.

There was a guy and a girl in an elevator.

She looks at him from head to toe, licks her lips provocatively, and stops the elevator. She takes off her blouse and mini skirt,

leaving only her bra and bikini, goes to him and whispers in his ear:
-Make me feel like a woman!
He looks at her from head to toe, takes off his jacket, shirt, and pants, hands them to her, and says:
-Wash and iron them!

A woman didn't want to marry her daughter to Abdul.

Trying to make him change his mind, she says:
-If you want to marry my daughter, bring her a Mercedes.
-Abdul loves, Abdul wants, Abdul brings Mercedes!
Abdul brings the Mercedes, the mother, desperate, tries again:
-My daughter will only marry you if you buy her villas in the mountains and by the sea.
-Abdul loves, Abdul wants, Abdul buys villas!
Abdul buys the villas, and the mother has one last idea:
-My daughter can only marry someone who is 30 centimeters long!
-Abdul loves, Abdul wants, Abdul cuts!

In a training plane for parachutists, a group of beginners

was huddled in fear on the bench, wearing all their equipment and helmets. The instructor comes and asks:
-Well, are you scared?
The parachutists remain silent, trembling with fear. The instructor opens the trapdoor they were supposed to jump from and urinates through it. The parachutists remain silent, still trembling. The instructor calls the first parachutist to stand near the trapdoor. The parachutist approaches, trembling, and adjusts the parachute harness between his legs. The instructor asks:
-Does it bother your balls?
-Yes, the parachutist responds.
-Get out of here, coward!
The second parachutist comes, and the instructor asks:
-Does it bother your balls?
-Yes.
-Get out of here, coward!
Several more go through the same routine, and at one point:
-Does it bother your balls?
-No.
-No? No.
-This is a model parachutist, says the instructor, this is an example of courage to be followed by all. Tell me, what's your name?
-Mary!

Who am I?

I am a common object, pleasing to both sexes, about 18 centimeters long, with small bristles at one end and a hole at the other. Most of the day, I lie down, but I'm always ready for action. When used, I move back and forth in a warm and wet hole. When the job is done, there remains a shiny, white foam, and then I return to the original position. Usually, after that, there's a cleaning. Who am I?

I am your toothbrush, what did you think?

A big boss goes to the doctor and says:

–Doctor, my testicles are turning black.
The doctor takes a liquid from a bottle and cleans the boss' testicles. After a while, the boss goes back to the doctor.
–Doctor, my testicles are turning black again.
The doctor cleans his testicles again with the liquid, but this time he tells him:
–And tell your secretary not to wipe her ass with indigo paper.

President Bush and Secretary of State Colin Powell were sitting in a bar.

A guy walks in and asks the bartender:

-Isn't that President Bush and Colin Powell over there, at the table?
-Yes, they are, replies the bartender.
-So the guy goes to them and says:
-What an honor, what are you doing here?
-We're planning the third world war, says Bush.
-Seriously? What's going to happen?
-We're going to kill 140 million Iraqis and a blonde with big boobs, says Bush.
To which the guy responds:
-A blonde with big boobs? Why a blonde with big boobs?
Bush turns to Powell, pats him on the shoulder and says:
- You see, smart guy, I told you nobody cares about 140 million Iraqis!

A man from Arkansas comes home early from the field and hears noises in the bedroom.

He rushes in and finds his wife completely naked, lying on the bed, sweaty and panting...
-What's wrong, wife? What happened?
-I'm having a heart attack, she says.
-The man is about to run outside to call the doctor when his 4-year-old child says:
-Daddy, daddy, Uncle George is under the bed, completely naked...
The man rushes back, lifts the blanket, sees George under the bed naked, and says:
-Well, you scumbag, my wife is having a heart attack and you're running around the house naked scaring my child...

A ragged man walks into a bank.

At the counter, he says to the teller:
-Miss, I want to deposit some shitty money in your shitty bank...
-Sir, we don't allow such language in our bank. Let me call the manager.
-What's the problem, sir? the manager asks.
-I told the miss here that I want to deposit some shitty money in your shitty bank...
-What's the amount in question?
-A shitty amount of about two million dollars...
-And this whore doesn't want to serve you?

Two old women are talking about their husbands:

-Mary, my George is 100% impotent!
-Lena, my John is 300% impotent!
-How come?
The fool fell down the stairs and broke his fingers and bit his tongue!

A guy is sitting in a hotel bar and sees an attractive woman

at another table. He calls the waiter and asks him to invite her to join him. The waiter returns:
-The lady said she can't come because she has new prosthetic legs that squeak, but maybe you would like to go to her table!
The guy goes, they talk, and in the end, he invites her to his hotel room. The woman refuses, still citing the squeaking prosthetic legs, and invites him to the bushes instead. They go to the bushes, the guy holds her legs under his arm, and they start... Two drunkards, even drunker:
-Look, man! He's drunker than us! He's doing it with a scarecrow!

Lawyer: Did you have sexual relations with him in New York?

Witness: I refuse to answer that question.
Lawyer: Did you have sexual relations with him in Chicago?
Witness: I refuse to answer that question.
Lawyer: Did you have sexual relations with him in Miami?
Witness: No.

An old man goes to the doctor.

The doctor asks him:
-How are your heart and lungs? Very well.
-But is there something bothering you?
-Yes, I have a problem: when I have sex, I hear whistling in my ears.
-How old are you?
-83 years old.
-Well, at 83, what would you expect to hear, applause?

An old couple is sitting as usual for breakfast on the terrace.

The wife leans over the table and smacks her husband on the back of his chair. After a moment of silence, the old man asks, surprised:
-What the hell was that for?
-For 45 years of unsuccessful sex.
He sinks into deep thought in his chair. After a while, he gets up and smacks her on the head, causing her to fly off the terrace along with the chair.
-And why did you do that? she screams at him.
- How do you know the difference between successful and unsuccessful sex?

A guy picks up a girl and, not having anywhere to take her,

takes her to the bushes in the nearby park. Without much hesitation, he starts having sex with her vigorously. The girl says:
-I want more!
He does it again, but at the end, the girl comes up with the same request... The poor man repeats the action 4-5 more times, with the same result! Barely able to stand on his feet, he tells her to take a walk on the path for a while, catch some breath, and he will come back to start over. On the deserted paths of the park, he spots a lonely passerby:
-Man, wait a moment, let me tell you something. Look, I met this girl, I brought her here, we did it six times and I can't do it anymore. Help me out, come in my place since it's dark and she won't notice... Don't be mad, it's just between us guys.
-Is she hot?
-She's hot, very good, and she knows everything...
The passerby goes into the bushes, starts the job with determination, when a policeman appears with a flashlight:
-Ahhh... I caught you... What are you doing here?
-Well... I'm fixing my wife...
-Oh, excuse me... I didn't know...
-Well... me neither until you turned on the flashlight...

At the end of a long and dark tunnel, the young man says to the girl:

-This tunnel cost 9 million dollars!
-It was worth it, says the girl, fixing her hair...

Two thugs break into the bedroom of the nuns at a monastery.

From the darkness, one of the nuns speaks:
-Forgive him, Lord, for he doesn't know what he's doing!
-Shut up, says the nun next to her, mine knows...

A guy approaches a girl in a bar:

-Do you want to play Magic?
-What's that?
-We go to my place, have sex, and then you disappear.

A driver on the highway picks up a hot chick in his car.

Naturally, his hand keeps slipping off the gearshift onto the girl's legs. Just as they enter the city, the girl, incredibly aroused, says:
-I want to do it!

-Have a little patience, we'll be at my place in fifteen minutes and we can do it then!
-No, I want it now! If we don't do it right here, I'll scream, yell, and jump out while the car is moving!
-Poor guy, what could he do? He stops the car, lifts it with a jack, puts a blanket underneath, and starts.
Suddenly, he feels a tap on his shoulder.
-What do you want, man? Can't you see I'm busy?
The tapping on the shoulder repeats. When the man looks, it's a policeman.
-Good day, officer!
-Sir, the policeman says, what you're doing here is your business, but it's my duty to inform you that your car has been stolen for the past fifteen minutes...

-What's easier to give up: wine or women?

-It depends on their age...

A woman goes to the animal market.

She wants to surprise her husband.
-Good day, ma'am!
-Good day, I would like a parrot.
-Unfortunately, we only have one parrot left. It used to live in a brothel, but it's very cute.

The woman buys it. At home, she covers it up and waits for her beloved husband. The husband arrives home, enters the room, and the wife removes the cloth from the cage. The parrot looks around and says:
–Hm... new room, hm... new bed, hm... new whore. Hello, George!

Santa Claus enters through the chimney into a house

and ends up in the bedroom of a gorgeous young woman who was sleeping naked in bed. Indecisive, he starts wandering around the room, saying:
–If I do it, I won't be welcomed in heaven anymore, but if I don't do it, I won't be able to get out through the chimney.

What's the difference between a woman and a man?

–A woman needs only one man to fulfill all her desires. A man needs all women to fulfill his one desire...

A young woman tells her friend:

-On Sunday, at the beach, guys hit on me just because I was wearing my swimsuit in a funny way.
-What do you mean? How were you wearing it?
-In my hand...

A blind man comes to the beach and starts inflating an object.

After a few minutes, people around him start getting agitated. Finally, someone gathers the courage and goes to him:
-Sir, don't get upset! Do you know that this is an inflatable woman?
-Oh no! It means I spent the whole winter f*cking the air mattress.

A very handsome and well-dressed guy enters a bar

and sits at the bar counter next to a very attractive girl. He quickly glances at her, then looks at his watch very carefully and attentively. The girl notices the look he gave her and asks:
-Is your watch running slow?
-I don't think so. I just bought a masterpiece of a watch that cost me a fortune, and now I wanted to test it...
-And what's so special about your expensive watch?

Well, for example, it now tells me that you're not wearing any panties at the moment.
The girl starts laughing and says:
-Your watch is lying because I am wearing panties right now!
-Oh, for God's sake! It's already one hour ahead!

Two deaf-mutes get married.

In the first week, they realize that they can only communicate in the bedroom with the lights on, as they understood each other through sign language. After several nights of misunderstandings, the wife comes up with a solution:
-Honey, she explains through signs, can't we decide on some simple signals? For example, if you want to have sex one night, squeeze my right breast once. If you don't want to have sex, squeeze my left breast once.
The husband is very excited:
- Likewise, if you want to have sex, pull my penis once. If you don't want to have sex, pull it 50 times quickly, and the last 3 times faster.

A cute girl enters a pharmacy and asks the pharmacist:

-Do you have extra-large condoms for sale?

-Of course we do. Do you want to buy them?
-No, but do you mind if I wait here until someone comes to buy them?

It's summertime and very hot.

The husband comes out of the shower naked and says to his wife:
-Honey, I need to mow the lawn. What do you think the neighbors will say if I go outside naked?
-They'll probably think I married you for your money...

A man goes to the pharmacy to buy condoms.

-What size do you need? asks the pharmacist.
-I didn't know they came in sizes. How can I find out my size? the man asks.
The pharmacist hands him a wooden instrument with several round holes of different sizes and says:
-We have this instrument. Take it to the back, insert your penis into each hole, and find out which size fits you.
After 10 minutes, the man comes out and says:
-Forget about the condoms! How much does the instrument cost?

The lion, in the jungle, gathers all the animals and says:

-Whoever has the courage to jump from the highest cliff in the jungle can have a night with my lioness.
All the animals climb up to the top of the cliff, while the lion stays below. Suddenly, a small black dot is seen, the dot gets bigger and bigger until the bear lands. The lion approaches him and says:
-Congratulations, bear! For your courage, you can have my lioness for a night.
The bear says:
-Lioness, lioness. But wait until you see what I'll do to the one who pushed me off the cliff!

After winter, the bear comes out of hibernation very horny and says:

-The first animal that crosses my path, I'll catch and f*ck it!
The first animal that crosses his path is the hedgehog, who, when he sees the bear, hides inside his spiky shell. The bear grabs him, turns him around, and says:
-Where's the hole, huh?
-Give up, I'm too small, and you won't be able to do anything to me, says the hedgehog.
-Oh, you spoke. Where did you speak from?

-You crazy person, why did you sell the table?

-Because you cheated on it...
-If you were to go by that, only the doorbell would remain in the house...

-Hey, George, what gift should I get you for your birthday?

-Mary, my dear, just love me and be faithful, that's all I want.
-Well, it's too late, I bought you socks!

-My wife was a magician's assistant for many years and learned some good tricks from him.

-For example, on Fridays, I come home from work, walk into the bedroom, she sees me and shouts:
-Abracadabra!
-And suddenly, guess what?

-My friend, Ronnie, comes out naked from the closet.
-I laughed so hard, poor guy, I felt sorry for him. I think he was wondering how he ended up naked in my closet!

-It was horrible, Mom, Mary complains.

I had to change seats four times at the cinema.
-Did any man hit on you?
-Eventually, yes...

Honey, I'm pregnant!

-We're going to have 37.5 children!!
-You're so dumb, you peed on the thermometer...

At an art exhibition, a visitor was deeply offended

because he was standing in front of a painting titled "George in Prague" which depicted a woman engaging in wild lovemaking with three men simultaneously. He addresses the curator:

—I understand that in modern art, paintings have strange titles, but the title of this painting is totally absurd. What does it have to do with George?
—The woman in the painting is actually George's wife, explains the curator.
—Well, where is George then?
—The title tells you, he's gone to Prague.

A mosquito has been sucking my blood for about 10 minutes.

Out of reflex, I started petting its head.

Did you know that there are no canaries in the Canary Islands?

It's the same with the Virgin Islands, no canaries there either.

A 70-year-old shepherd marries a 15-year-old girl.

On their wedding night, the old man undresses and gets into bed. The girl hesitates to undress. The old man asks her,
-What happened? Why aren't you undressing?
The girl replies,
- Well, sir, I'm embarrassed because I haven't grown hair down there yet.
The old man then says,
- Don't worry, my dear, by the time I get an erection, your hair will have grown too!

Husband and wife in bed at night.

The husband starts caressing his wife with intention, but she says, "Not tonight, darling, because tomorrow I have an appointment with the gynecologist and I want to be fresh."
The disappointed husband withdraws, but after 5 minutes, he gets an idea:
 - Darling, do you happen to have a dentist appointment too?

In a passenger plane, the pilots were talking to each other in the cockpit.

Unfortunately, they forgot to turn off the microphone and all the passengers could hear what they were saying. At one point, one of the pilots says:
-See that flight attendant? After I finish this coffee, I'm going to have sex with her.
Upon hearing this, the flight attendant rushes to the cockpit to tell the pilots to close the microphone. Seeing her in a hurry, an elderly passenger says:
-Why are you in such a hurry, dear? Let the man finish his coffee!

A bank robbery.

The robbers enter the bank wearing masks. One of the robbers approaches the cashier and orders:
-Get on your knees and suck my d**k!!
The cashier says:
-No, I can't. You came to take the money, what else do you want?
The robber:
-Get on your knees or I'll kill you! And he puts the gun to her head.
With no other choice, the cashier starts doing it, to which the robber says:
-That's it, honey, see, it's possible!

A man goes hunting in the forest and encounters a bear.

The bear says to him:
-I'm the brown bear, and since you've entered my territory, you have two options. Either I kill you or I rape you.
The man, thinking that he might survive the rape, agrees to be violated. He spends a month in the hospital and then goes hunting again. He encounters the bear once more, who says the same thing:
-I'm the brown bear, and since you've entered my territory, you have two options. Either I kill you or I rape you.
Once again, the man agrees to be violated and spends two months in the hospital. After recovering, he goes hunting again. He meets the bear once more, who says:
-Hey, isn't it true that you're not here for hunting?

Gigel's parents want to have sex but don't know what to do with the child.

However, the man has an idea:
-Johnny, go out on the balcony and tell us what's happening outside. Johnny goes out on the balcony and starts narrating:
-Mr. Thompson from the ground floor took his dog to a bush to pee... A police officer is looking for something... Mrs. Jane just left with her boyfriend... Georgie's parents are at it...

-How do you know all that? the father asks from the other room.
-He's alone on the balcony, just like me.

A lady calls the carpenter to locate and fix an annoying noise

she hears in her house. He comes and asks:
- How come I don't hear anything now?
- It's not always there, only when the bus passes by on the street.
- And where do you hear it from?
- From the closet.
- Alright, I'll go into the closet, and when the bus passes by, I'll figure out what it is.
Said and done. But after a few minutes, the lady's husband comes home in a hurry to change because he has an important meeting. He opens the closet and finds himself face to face with the carpenter. To which the carpenter says:
- If I tell you I'm waiting for the bus, would you believe me...?

In the evening, at the zoo, in front of the monkey enclosure.

A boy and girl are caressing each other. An orangutan, fed up, stands at the bars and watches them.

Guy: Let's try something! Open your blouse a little and let's see how he reacts. The woman obediently follows her man's request and unbuttons the first buttons of her blouse. The

orangutan's eyes widen, its tongue is hanging out, and it starts jumping in circles, making typical primate movements, inside its cage.
Guy: Further... further. Lift your skirt a little... The very obedient woman lifts her skirt a bit, and a well-shaped leg sees the light of day. The orangutan can't take it anymore: with its tongue out, bulging eyes, screaming and shaking, it tries to bend the bars.
The guy opens the cage door and pushes the woman into the arms of the orangutan, saying:
- Well, now explain to him that you have a migraine!!

Great excitement at the circus.

An extraordinary animal training act: the huge crocodile opens its mouth, its trainer unzips his pants, takes out his penis, and puts it in the animal's mouth, then hits it on the head with a baton.
The animal quickly closes its powerful jaws.
Everyone is stunned.
After a while, the animal opens its mouth again, and the trainer's penis appears intact between the sharp teeth. The applause and cheers don't stop. The trainer says:
- Dear spectators, whoever among you has the courage to repeat the act I just performed will receive ten thousand dollars.
No one volunteers, except for a woman from the back row.

- I would try, she says. But I have one request. Please don't hit me too hard with the baton!

A sociology student is working on his doctoral thesis.

To conduct his research, he has to live on a sheep farm for two months and observe the shepherds' habits.
At the beginning of the first month, he notices that the shepherds satisfy their sexual desires with the sheep. He laughs at them, but by the end of the month, he can no longer bear the "celibacy" himself. One evening, the shepherds catch him in the act with an ewe. And they start laughing.
- Why are you laughing? You do it with the sheep too, don't you? says the student.
- Yes, but not with that damn slut.

In a dormitory, two guys go to the showers

but realize they forgot their soaps. One of them goes back to the room completely naked to get two soaps. In the hallway, he meets three female students. To avoid embarrassment, he pretends to be a statue. The girls reach him and start spinning and looking at him.
- What is this? one of them asks.
The second one, looking at the guy's penis, says:
- Maybe we should pull this handle.

- She pulls it, and the guy drops a soap.
- Ah, look, it's a soap dispenser, says the first girl.
- Oh, let me try, says the second one and pulls it as well, until the guy drops the second soap.

- Now it's my turn, says the third student and keeps pulling and pulling, but the poor guy has no more soap to drop. The girl keeps pulling, and at some point, she says:
- Look, it's also distributing liquid soap!

A lady doctor is stuck in the snow with her car on a mountain.

John and George are leaning on their shovels, watching without doing anything.
Doctor: Hey, good people, help me too!
John looks at George, George looks at John.
John: Doctor, we'll help you, but we're going to f**k you.
After some hesitation, the doctor agrees:
- Alright, good people, but please wear these on top because I don't want to get pregnant.
They get the job done, they dig the car out of the snow, and the doctor leaves.
Two days later, John says to George:
- Hey, I don't know if the doctor will get pregnant or not, but I'm taking off the rubber because I have to pee!

A wife goes to court and files for divorce.

The reason: her husband doesn't satisfy her anymore. During the hearing, the judge asks the husband:

- Why don't you fulfill your marital obligations?
- Well, Your Honor, I do fulfill them because I have 35 cm.
- Then, what more do you expect, woman? the judge asks the wife.
- Well, deduct 15 cm from my belly, 15 cm from his belly, and if you have 5 cm left of the tool...

Two guys, a husband and wife, are at a nudist beach.

Suddenly, a bee flies into the woman's vagina. Desperate, the husband takes her to a nearby clinic. There, the doctor explains to the man:
- I'll apply honey on your penis, you'll insert it into her vagina, and when you feel the bee has settled on it, quickly pull it out. But due to the man's great fear, his penis doesn't get erect at all. So the doctor asks if he can try instead. The man, fearing that the bee might sting his wife in such a delicate place, agrees. The doctor applies honey on his penis, and it instantly becomes monstrously erect. He inserts it into the woman's vagina and waits. Seeing that nothing is happening, he starts moving his penis. The confused man asks:
- What are you doing, doctor?
To which the doctor replies:
- Change of plan, I'm drowning the damn bee!

A priest asks John to help him dig a hole. The priest says:

- John, go to my house and bring those two shovels!
- Alright, Father!

John goes into the house where the priest's two daughters are and says:
- The Father told me to f*ck you!
- That's not true! one of them says.

John opens the window and shouts:
- Both of them, Father?
- Both of them!

John's parents go to Mary's parents to arrange the wedding,

which will take place in two weeks. In the evening, John and Mary stand at the gate as a young couple. They hug, kiss, tease each other, and at some point, John says:
- Mary, let's do it! What's the difference between now and two weeks from now? You're still my woman.
- John, no. When we come out of the altar, I'll be all yours, but until then, nothing.
- Alright, but at least show it to me so I can see it!

Mary lifts her skirt and says:
- Well, here it is!

John gets closer, looks, wrinkles his nose, and says:

- Mary, it's a must now because based on the smell, it won't last two weeks.

An old woman trembling from every joint

asks the saleswoman at the Sex Shop:
- Do you have the Turbo XXL Super Strong Vibrator with alkaline batteries?
- Yes!
- And how do you turn it off?

At a conference on the topic of Sex Around the World,

the room is full. A somewhat elderly and frail lecturer appears and starts directly:
- As you know, there are 999 ways to have sex in the world...
A voice from the audience:
- A thousand!
Visibly annoyed, the lecturer stops:
- Please, a little decency, we are discussing serious matters here! So, as I was saying, there are 999 ways to have sex in the world...
From the audience:
- A thousand!

- Gentlemen, if you don't stop, I will end the conference here! Please!
Silence in the room. He continues:
- In the world, there are 999 ways to have sex... He stops to see if anyone will interrupt him. Silence in the room.

- The first way: the man on top and the woman underneath...
From the audience:
- A thousand and one, because I didn't know that one!

Two friends are waiting for the Japanese subway

(known to be very crowded), commenting enthusiastically on the guys around them. The subway arrives, and the two are simply squeezed into the crowded subway and end up facing each other, unable to turn around. One of them asks the other:
- How's the guy?
- Young.
- I can tell, but what does he look like?!

At the office, the secretaries and typists are tired of the sexually suggestive jokes their bosses make about them,

so they decide that the next time it happens, they will all leave the office.

The next day, the personnel director shows up:
- Ladies, have you heard that a whole ship of sex-starved sailors has arrived at the port?... Oh, wait, where are you all rushing like this? The ship will stay for a week!

On the Titanic, after the impact, a guy takes a lifeboat and rows desperately to save himself.

- Where are you going alone, there are still women here? a man asks. The guy replies:
- Leave me alone, man, I'm in the mood for f*cking now!

In a train, a guy and a girl were sitting face to face.

The girl, incredibly hot, thighs, breasts, miniskirt, no panties. The guy was trying hard not to stare between her legs. The girl notices and says:
- I see you're looking at my p*ssy. Do you like it?!!!
The guy blushes:
- Well... um... no...
- Never mind, it's no problem, I enjoy it... Tell me, do you want my pussy to blow you a kiss?
- Well... Yes!!
The girl spreads her legs and her pussy, very naturally, blows de guy a kiss. The guy is ecstatic:
- Super awesome!!!

- But wait, you want to see something even better? Do you want my pussy to blink?
- Absolutely...
- And the pussy blinks a few times...
The guy thrilled to the max:
- Wow!!!

- Come closer to me, she says. Do you want to put two fingers into my pussy?!!
The guy says astonished:
- Oh, don't tell me it can whistle too!!!

Pensioners are chatting:

- Christmas is the best holiday.
- But having sex is more enjoyable!
- True, but Christmas comes more often.

Smith goes to the doctor and says:

- Doctor! My penis is always standing upright! At first, I liked it, but now it's gone too far!
The doctor examines him and with a pair of tweezers removes an ant, shows it to him, and says:
- This was the cause!
- Doctor! I am incredibly grateful to you. What do I owe you?

- Nothing, but the ant stays here!

The rabbit decides to go to a brothel.

He goes there, approaches the madam, and says:
- Please, I want the best girl you have here. Look, I have money, everything is fine.
- Well, rabbit, it doesn't work like that. In order to have the best girl, you need to be something extraordinary, a Superman. Have you been training recently?
- Not really, says the rabbit, but we rabbits, you know, we are virile.
- It doesn't work like that, go, train yourself, then we'll talk.
The rabbit goes and trains for a whole month, practicing his skills on tree hollows. He comes back and says:
- I'm ready, I've trained, give me the best one.
- Alright, rabbit, if you say so, fine, see that room over there.
The rabbit goes in, and all the women are curious, thinking, "What's the deal with this guy who asked for the best and even trained for it? Let's listen and see what's going on." They gather around the door, and they can hear the woman screaming in horror.
- Look at that, the others say, the rabbit is really something, listen to what he's doing.
When they look through the keyhole, they see the rabbit holding the woman by her legs and shaking her vigorously. They all burst into the room:
- What are you doing, you scoundrel, you pervert, what's with these things?
- Well, you see, says the rabbit calmly, in the forest on hollow trees, I've had encounters with bees before.

A very shy guy enters a bar and sees a beautiful young woman sitting at the bar.

After an hour, mustering up all the courage he needs, he finally goes up to her and says:
- Do you mind if we talk for a bit?|
Upon hearing this, the woman shouts at the top of her lungs, -
- No, I'm not going to sleep with you tonight! Aren't you ashamed?
Everyone in the bar now turns their attention to the two of them. Naturally, the guy is overwhelmed with embarrassment and timidly returns to his table. After a few minutes, the woman approaches him and apologizes. She smiles at him and says:
- I'm sorry if I made you feel bad. You know, I'm a psychology student, studying people's reactions in embarrassing situations. To which the guy responds loudly:
- What? $200 for a blowjob??!!! You whore!!!

John and Mary in bed...

Passionate moments... She says:
- Take me, be wild, show me you're a real man!
Him: - Yes! Yes! Yes!
Her: - Tell me dirty things!
Him: - Bathroom, kitchen, living room carpet.

The bear and the rabbit are driving in a car.

A fox, hitchhiking, asks:
- Can I ride with you?
- Sure!
When it's time for her to get off, the fox asks:
- Do you want money or shall I pay you in nature?
- How in nature?
- Well, you know, I take off my panties, and...
After careful consideration, the bear says:
- I prefer money!
The fox shrugs, pays, and leaves. After some more intellectual efforts, the bear says:
- Well, rabbit, I did well by asking for money and not payment in nature; those panties were too small for me, but too big for you!

A rocker is walking through the desert.

God sees him and thinking, He descends to Earth in the form of a man. He goes to the rocker and asks him to accompany him to the first oasis. As they walk, the rocker takes out a loaf of bread and hands him half of it. They keep walking, and the rocker takes out a bottle of vodka and shares it with God. Near the oasis, the rocker takes out a joint and shares it with the man (God). Impressed, God tells him the truth, to which the rocker says:
- This weed is strong, dude!

In the Wild West of America, in a bar...

a voice is heard... "Billy-Boy is coming..."
Everyone runs wherever they can, hiding under tables...
One guy rushes into the bar in a hurry and goes straight to the bartender and says,
- Quick, suck my d**k... as fast as you can... as fast as possible... do it now!
The bartender complies... and the guy leaves... The same thing happens the next day... and the next... and the fourth day as well... After finishing the task, the bartender asks the suspect,
- Why do you want it so fast?
To which the man replies:
- Can't you hear? Billy-Boy is coming!

A stingy person calls a hot line.

On the other end of the line, the voice says:
- Darling, welcome, I'll do anything you want, however you want it, whenever you want it!
The stingy person asks:
- Do you really do everything I want?
- Yes, darling, everything you want, however you want it, whenever you want it.
- Then I'm hanging up, and you call me.

The village priest goes to the local police station and complains:

- My dear son, help me, my bicycle has been stolen. What should I do?
- What should you do, Father? During the Sunday service, when you mention the Ten Commandments, look around carefully because the one who hides is the thief.

After the service, the priest goes to the police officer.
- May God bless you, my son, I found my bicycle.
- Did it happen as I told you?
- Almost... I started listing the commandments, and when I reached "Thou shalt not commit adultery," I immediately remembered where I left it.

- John, get yourself a bigger swimsuit! Your whole thing is hanging out.

The man responds, offended:
- The whole thing? Only half of it!

On their wedding night, the young couple retreats to the bedroom,

and she tells her new husband:
- My love, it's time to tell you something... I don't know how to

do anything, I have no idea.
- Don't worry, my dear. Undress, lie down on your back, relax, spread your legs, and I'll take care of the rest.
_ Oh, no, you little fool... I know how to have sex... I was referring to cooking, washing, ironing.

One day, a guy takes a girl into a bedroom,

undresses her, and gets ready to get on top of her. But before that, he asks:
- Hey, miss, how old are you?
- 13
- Oh nooo!! Quickly, gather your clothes and run!
She looks at him oddly:
- Wow, sir, I didn't know you were so superstitious!

Conversation between two women:

- Why are you so tired, my dear?
It's because of my husband...
- What does he do?

- Well, he wakes up in the morning, we make love, he goes to the bathroom... comes back, and we make love again, he eats, and it's the same thing again... And so it goes all day...
- And haven't you taken him to the doctor?
- Yes, and the doctor told me he's forgetting things.

The husband comes home and finds his wife with a lover.

He takes out his gun, saying:
- Come with me.
The husband proposes to the lover:
- Let's do it this way: I'll shoot twice in the air, and we both fall to the ground. Whichever of us my wife approaches first, that person can stay with her.
The wife hears two gunshots. She looks out the window, then shouts:
- John, come out from under the bed. They shot each other!

An 80-year-old man goes to the doctor.

- Doctor, I'm getting married tomorrow!
- Well, old man, how old is the bride?
- She's 21...
- I have to warn you, any sexual activity could be fatal!
The old man thinks for a moment and says,
- Well, if she dies... she dies!

Dad, can you lend us the car, me and my boyfriend?

- I have no gasoline left in the tank, my dear.
- No problem, we weren't planning on leaving the garage with it anyway.

A woman is sunbathing on the beach without a bra.

Her magnificent breasts catch the attention of a man. He keeps looking and eventually tries to start a conversation with her:
- Can you tell me how warm the water is?
- Listen, sir! She replies irritated. Many people have mistaken me for a prostitute, but no one has ever mistaken me for a thermometer.

Two friends at the hair salon:

- Darling, let me tell you what happened to me yesterday: I was coming back from the market, a guy behind me. I reach the front of the building, the guy is still behind me. I enter the elevator, he follows me, I get out of the elevator, he gets out too, I reach my apartment door, he's still behind me, I go inside, he follows without saying anything, takes me to the bedroom, and has sex with me.

- And what did you say?
- Well... if he didn't say anything, what was I supposed to say?

At the gynecologist's office, a frightened young woman:

- Doctor, disaster!... I was playing with a vibrator, and it got stuck inside me. What should I do?
- Please lie down here!
- The woman lies down, the doctor examines her for a moment, then says:
- Miss, I have two news for you, one is good, and one is bad. Which one should I start with?
- Start with the bad news, the woman says anxiously.
- The bad news is that I couldn't remove the vibrator from you.
- And the good news?
- I managed to change the battery.

One evening, a husband and wife return from a wedding.

Climbing the stairs behind her, he says to his wife:
- Honey, you have a butt as big as a washing machine!
When they are about to go to bed, he feels in the mood and asks her for sex. To which she, annoyed, responds:

- I'm not going to start the washing machine for such a small load! You could just wash it by hand.

The rabbit systematically beats the wolf at chess, so the wolf gets angry and asks:

- Hey, little rabbit, how come you beat me every time?
- Wolf, the secret is that I always have sex before playing.
- The next day, the wolf goes to the kitchen to find his wife and grabs her waist, determined to take her to the bedroom. Feeling him behind her, the she-wolf exclaims:
- Oh, oh, are you going to play chess again, little rabbit?

Why were men invented?

Because, for now, they haven't invented a vibrator that can fix the TV.

A grandfather was sitting on a bench in the park with his grandson.

The grandson asks his grandfather:
- Grandpa, do you take Viagra?
- No, my dear.
- Why not?
- Well, you see... what's the point of sharpening the pencil if you have no one to write to?

What is the difference between masturbating and having sex?

In principle, there is no difference, but if you have sex, you get to know more people.

What is the advantage of having group sex?

If you have things to do, you can leave.

Two teenagers are deeply in love for a few weeks,

but the boy is unhappy because she doesn't want to quit smoking. One afternoon, after a passionate lovemaking session, she lights up a cigarette.
- Sweetheart, I really think you should quit smoking, he tells her seriously.
Tired of all the nagging, she responds with boredom:
- But I really enjoy a good cigarette after sex.
- Well, didn't you know that cigarettes slow down the body's development?
Then she asks him if he has ever smoked in his life. He replies that no, he has never even tried it. With a mischievous grin on her face, she asks again:
- Alright, so what's your excuse then?

A boy and a girl spend a hot night of passion together.

At one point, as they lie side by side on the bed, the girl exclaims:
- Thank goodness, I finally did it! I'm not a virgin anymore!
The boy, upon hearing this, asks:
- Are you saying that I was the first?
- Well... I wanted to wait until I found a man I truly loved.
- So, does that mean you love me? he responds, amazed.
- Oh, no... Heavens, no... the girl says. I just got tired of waiting for so long!

On their wedding night, the bride says to her groom:

– My dear, you know I'm a virgin and I don't know much about sex. Could you explain it to me before we proceed?
– Alright, my love. Let's imagine that my private part is a prisoner, and yours is a prison. It's really simple: we take the prisoner and put him in the prison. So they do. After the act, the groom lies in bed, satisfied with himself. The bride, smiling happily and pleased with her first intimate experience, gently announces:
– Darling, it seems that the prisoner has escaped from the prison.
– Then we must arrest him again.
The man complies, and in the end, he tries to rest. The bride, radiating with satisfaction, softly says again:
– Sweetheart, the prisoner has escaped again.
Gathering his last bit of strength, the man rises and resumes the act. After finishing, all he wants is a good night's sleep. The bride gently taps his shoulder and says:
– Honeyyy, he escaped again...
– My dear, you know what?! That's not a life sentence!

A guy complains to his friend

about how his intimate life with his wife has become extremely boring and asks for advice in this regard.
– Buddy, you need to be creative! his friend responds. Why

don't you play doctor with her for about an hour?
- Sounds good, what can I say... but how do I manage to make that last for a whole hour?
- Nothing easier, his friend tells him. You keep her in the waiting room for 45 minutes!

I don't know what to do with you,

whether to bite you, suck you, lick you from top to bottom, or share you with friends... Delta ice cream.

The bunny smoked some weed and now lies flat on the edge of the lake.

A beaver appears:
- What are you doing, bunny?
- I smoked some weed and I feel like I'm in the twelfth heaven! Take some from here!
The beaver takes a puff. The bunny gets an idea:
- You know what would be even greater, beaver? Take a puff, hold your breath, dive, swim to the other side of the lake, and exhale there!
The beaver follows the instructions. On the other side of the lake, it falls down in pleasure. A hippopotamus appears:
- What are you doing, beaver?
The beaver explains what and how.

- There's a bunny on the other side of the lake with some amazing stuff. Hold your breath, swim underwater, and when you reach the other side, you'll find him.
The hippopotamus follows suit. When it emerges on the other side, the bunny looks at it with wide eyes and yells like crazy:
- Exhale, beaver!!! Didn't I tell you to exhale?!

A bunny wanted to make some pancakes.

He had ingredients for 20 pancakes but didn't have a frying pan to make them in. He decides to borrow one from the bear. On the way, he was thinking:
"If the bear asks me why I need the frying pan, I'll tell him I want to make 20 pancakes. And if he wants 5 too?
No problem. I'm small, 15 are enough for me, it's not enough for him because he's big. But if he wants 10?
No problem! I'm small, 10 are enough for me, it's not enough for him because he's big. But if he wants 15?" While he was thinking like that, he arrives at the bear's door and angrily tells him:
- Hey, bear! Do you have a frying pan?
- Yes! the bear replies.
- Well, f*ck you and your frying pan!

An old lady buys a pair of parrots

so she won't be alone in the house, but she has trouble telling them apart, so she calls the store. The salesman advises her to observe them for a while, and eventually, she'll know which one is the male parrot and which one is the female parrot. One day, the old lady catches them in the act... To not confuse them, she puts a white cardboard collar around the male parrot's neck.
After some time, a priest comes to visit the old lady. The parrot, after studying him for a moment, says to the priest:
- Looks like you've been caught doing it too...

When I went hunting in Africa, I encountered a lion.

I aimed my rifle and fired, but I missed. I kept shooting until I ran out of ammunition. Then I started running. The lion chased after me. Luckily, the lion slipped, and I managed to escape.
- If I were you, I would have shat myself.
- On what do you think the lion slipped?

In the dust on the edge of the road, a chicken digs persistently for worms.

A truck passes by and hits it.
The chicken lies in the dusty road for a while, then recovers and, shaking itself, says: "Now, that's a real cock!"

A woman goes to the gynecologist.

He asks her to undress.
- Where should I put my clothes?
- Here, next to mine.

A dog asks a cat:

- How come I've never seen cats making love in public?
- Do you want people to see us and steal our style, just like they did with you? the cat replied.

The bunny and his bunny girlfriend are being chased by several dogs.

At the last moment, they manage to hide in a hole in the ground. His girlfriend says:
- What do we do now?

- Very simple, says the bunny, we stay here until we outnumber them...

A fisherman catches the golden fish:

- Release me, fisherman, and I will grant you three wishes, but know that whatever you ask for, your neighbor, who has done me even more good, will receive double!

- No problem, as long as he's healthy! I want to have a palace in place of my shack!
- Poof! When the fisherman looked, he saw a grand palace in his yard, and his neighbor had two.
- I want a wife, someone I can look at like the sun, but he gets two!
- Poof! At the castle's doorstep stood an incredibly beautiful woman, and his neighbor had two.
- Little fish, here's my third wish: take away one of my testicles...!

Johnny arrives home one day and his dad sees that he has bruised eyes.

He asks:
- Johnny, why do you have bruised eyes?
- Well, you see: I was on the bus and I saw a girl with a skirt

stuck in her butt. I pulled it out, and that's how my eye got bruised.
- Alright, but what about the other eye?
- Well, I saw that she didn't like it, so I put it back in.

Johnny is born with a 40 cm long penis...

and as he grows up, he goes to the doctor.

- Doctor, can't you do anything about it? I have such a big thing, and all the women run away when I undress.
- Jonny, there's nothing I can do.
- But can't you cut some off?
- If I cut it, you'll die. But go to a witch, maybe she can cast a spell for you...
And Johnny goes angrily to the witch to have a spell done... After telling her his problem, the witch says:
- My little Johnny, there's nothing I can do, but go to the Black Mountain. In the cave, you'll find a frog. If she rejects your marriage proposal, she will reduce it by 10 cm.
So Johnny goes to the Black Mountain, crossing seas and lands... After he arrives, he goes to the cave and smears mud on his face so that the frog won't want him as a husband. He approaches her and stutters:
- F-frog, w-will you m-marry m-me?
The frog sees him and says:
- No!
Johnny happily goes away... On the way, he thinks that 30 cm is still too big, so he goes back to the frog.
- Will you marry me?
- I said no, and no, and no again!

Obama is signing autographs in a crowd of children.

One child says:
- My father says you intercept our phone calls and internet.
Obama:
- That's not your dad!

A woman goes on vacation to the Caribbean without her husband.

As soon as she arrives, she meets a handsome black man, and after a passionate night of love, she asks him:
- What's your name?
- I can't tell you, he replies.
Every evening they meet again, make love, and she asks him the same question, and he always gives the same answer. One evening she says:
- This is my last night here, I'm going home tomorrow. Will you finally tell me your name?
- I can't tell you, because you'll laugh at me, the black man says.
- Come on, I won't laugh, there's no reason to.
- Alright... My name is Snow.
The woman bursts into laughter, and the black man, furious, says:
- I knew you would laugh at me, I shouldn't have told you...!
- Nooo, I was just thinking that my husband won't believe me when I tell him that I had 30 cm of snow every day in the Caribbean!

Two apartment buildings facing each other.

The neighbors from the 5th floor go out to the balcony for a smoke. One of them calls the other and says:
- Neighbor, is your birthday on February 12th?
- Why?

- I want to buy you some blinds for your windows... I'm already tired of seeing you making love with your wife.
The other one asks:
- But when is your birthday? Is it on January 12th?
- Why? - asks the first one, intrigued.
- I want to gift you a telescope so you can see whose wife it is... mine or yours...

An American tourist visits London
when suddenly he feels the need to urinate. He looks around but can't find a restroom. With no other choice, he enters a dark alley, approaches a corner near a tall wall, and starts unzipping his pants.
Before he even starts urinating, he feels a light tap on his shoulder. He turns around, and there's a typical English policeman standing next to him.
- Excuse me, sir, says the policeman, but it's forbidden to urinate in public places.
The American apologizes, explaining that he had no choice, that he couldn't hold it anymore, and he couldn't find a

restroom.
- I'll help you, says the policeman, follow me.
He leads the tourist to a small door in the wall and shows him the way inside. The tourist enters, and his eyes almost pop out. He finds himself in a beautiful, well-maintained garden, full of grass, flowers, bushes, and trees.
The policeman points to one of the trees and says:
- No problem, you can urinate here. The American urinates, feeling relieved, and asks the policeman:
- Tell me, is this what they call English courtesy?
- No, replies the policeman, we call this the French Embassy...

"To err is human,"

said the heated hedgehog, getting off the black wire brush...

A city dweller visits his cousin who lives in the Arizona desert.

Suddenly, a howl is heard...
- What's that?
- Nothing, just the coyotes.
- But what are coyotes?
- Some wild dogs.
- And why are they howling like that?
- Well, we don't have trees here, only cacti!

Conversation between a cow and her calf:

– Alright, from today on, don't let Gigi catch you anymore!
– Why, Mom?
– That's why.
– Why?

– Well, his mom is a cow, and his dad is a pig.
– But, Mom, you're also a cow.
– Yes, but your father was a veterinarian...

A tomcat is heading home together with his girlfriend

after a night full of events. The tomcat can't contain himself and meows:
– Oh, my dear, I would die for you.
– The kitty gives him a seductive look and asks:
– Alright, but how many times?

Three bulls are standing on top of a hill,

casting longing glances at a herd of cows grazing in the valley.
– Quickly, quickly! Let's go down there and have our way with them, says the youngest of them.

– Well, well. Not so fast, young one! Have a little patience. First, we eat well, make ourselves handsome, and then we call the ladies to come up to us, says the second bull, slightly older than the first.
– Be serious. Why should we go down? Why should we call them? says the oldest of the bulls. We can see everything perfectly fine from up here.

I had everything a man could want:

a splendid apartment, a sports car, a motorcycle, a woman who loved me with all her being... Now, it's all gone... My wife found out.

While I was feeling my testicles, my wife comes up to me and asks:

– What are you doing?
– What do you think, I just read in a magazine that you have to check your testicles for lumps every day.
– And do you have to do it with your pants down? she asks me.
– Of course, I said.
– Right here in the market?

My wife entered my office for the first time today:

- So, this is where you work, John? she asks me.
Then, noticing a photograph on the desk of a voluptuous blonde, she points at it and asks:
- Who's that?
Seeing me starting to blush, my colleague George intervenes and says:
- John told us it's you!

Conversation between two cowboys:

- I find it immoral to meet your future wife in a bar!
- You're right. But how did you meet yours?
- I won her in a game of billiards!

She buys him a dozen underwear all in the same color.

Him: Why the same color? So people can say I never change my underwear?

Her: Which people?
Silence...

She returns unexpectedly and finds him in bed with... a dwarf lady.

- Well, you miserable jerk, didn't you swear just two weeks ago that you won't cheat on me anymore?
- Darling, I can't change all of a sudden... but as you can see, I'm trying to downsize.

Two friends are talking:

- I changed my gynecologist. I got a young one, he's always laughing and speaks very nicely.
- I won't change mine, he may be older, but you know how his hands tremble...

Lately, I was feeling more and more insecure

compared to my new girlfriend, so last night, wanting to regain some ground, I made a scene and said:
- Baby, I want you to talk as dirty as you can, impress me!
To which she replied:
- I want you to fuck me as hard as you can right now with your tiny cock!
- I'm not sure if that helped me much...

Two lesbians are walking down the street.

At some point, a sexy girl passes by. One of the lesbians says:
- Look at those long legs the girl has!
- Uh-huh!
- And those breasts! You can even see them from behind.
- Uh-huh!
- And that appetizing ass!
- Uh-huh!
- Why are you just saying "uh-huh"? Say something else.
The other lesbian takes out a piece of paper and writes on it:
- "I can't! My tongue got hard!"

A young man approaches a woman on the street:

– I have a question: if I offered you one million dollars, would you have sex with me? The answer comes immediately:
– Of course!
– And what about for 5 dollars?
– Oh, sir, what kind of woman do you think I am?
– That's already clear, now we're just negotiating the price!

Pessimist: – The women in this bar are all slutty.

Optimist: – I hope so too...

Having sex with my wife has depreciated like Coca-Cola.

"Cocaine", "Caffeine", "Light", and now "Zero".

Do you prefer blondes or brunettes?

- I prefer boobs...
- Okay, but what about hair color?
- I don't like boobs with hair...

Two friends who haven't seen each other in a long time meet at a bar.

One of them is struggling to hide the tears streaming down her face.
- What happened to you? the other asks.
- Nothing, I can't tell you!
- You're avoiding me, your best friend? Maybe I can help...
- What can you do? Now no one can help me anymore.
- But what happened?
- I just came back from a hunting trip in Africa.
- And?
- I was raped by a gorilla, the strongest male in the group...
- And?
- For five days, we had non-stop sex, continuously, without any breaks...
And she starts crying hysterically.

- Come on, try to calm down, her friend consoles her, at least you're alive. You're whole, that's what matters. I won't tell anyone, and that gorilla can't talk.
- Well, that's the thing, he doesn't talk, he doesn't write, he doesn't make phone calls, no emails, no text messages, nothing...

Before I left on vacation, my friends warned me:

- Be careful there in Thailand when you hook up with a woman... not all of them are what they seem.
So I met this beautiful woman... she looked like a woman, danced like a woman, kissed like a woman, but when she took me to her place and made a perfect parallel parking, I knew something was not right...

After having sex with a girl, a guy quickly rushes to his notebook and starts jotting something down.

The girl, upset, tells him:
- How rude of you, am I one of those to be listed in your notebook?
- I'm not listing you, he replies, I'm erasing you!

The husband catches his wife in bed with another man

and instead of doing anything else, he starts making the sign of the cross.
- Man, I swear I don't understand you! I'm her husband and I have my duties to fulfill, but what obligations do you have?

Sitting on a park bench in the evening, a boy and a girl.

The guy keeps touching her back constantly. Eventually, she asks:
- What are you doing?
- I'm looking for breasts.
- Breasts are in the front!
- I've already searched there.

Are you a virgin?

- Yes.
- I don't believe you, swear.
- I swear on my son's eyes...

Newlyweds. She says:

– Darling, all you think about all day is sex; couldn't we talk a little about art, about literature?
– Fine... have you read Balzac?
– No.
– Okay, then let's go to bed!

Neighbor, I'm devastated. My wife is cheating on me!

She told me last night that she slept at her friend Jenny.
– And?
– Well, I slept at Jenny's!

The first son comes home:

– Dad, give me five thousand dollars because I got a girl pregnant.
The second son arrives:
– Dad, give me seven thousand dollars because I got a girl pregnant.
The daughter comes in:
– Dad, I'm pregnant.
– Finally, some returns on investment!

The husband comes home very agitated:

– You whore! I know everything, absolutely everything!
– Calmly, the wife says:
– Really? Boasting as usual... In what year did the Battle of Somme take place?

Mommy, today on the bus, dad made me give up my seat for a lady...

– Very good, my dear, that's what you should do!
– Yes, mommy, but I was sitting on dad's lap...

Husband: Every time we argue, you remain very calm. How do you manage that?

Wife: I go and clean the toilet bowl.
Husband: And that calms you down?
Wife: Yes, because I clean it with your toothbrush!

The building manager says he has slept with all the women in the building, except for one...

It must be the fat and old lady on the ground floor.

In a crowded bus, a woman feels that a man is staring at her

and repeatedly touching her buttocks. Outraged, she asks him:
- Sir, don't you have anywhere else to put your hand?
- Well, yes, but I didn't dare...

A lesson in an agricultural institute.

A couple attends the class, and because they are having an argument, the woman sits in the front row, and the man in the back row. At one point, the professor says:
- A healthy bull should have up to 12 matings per day...
The woman in the front row:
- Excuse me, professor, how many?

- Up to 12.
- Please repeat that for the back row!
The man in the back row:
- Tell me, professor, is that with one cow or with 12?
- Of course, with 12.
- Thank you. Please repeat that for the front row...

Scheherazade tells her friends:

- Aladdin, the one with the magic lamp, visited me. He started rubbing, rubbing, and rubbing, and all my wishes came true!
- Your wishes were fulfilled by the Genie...
- Who said Aladdin brought the lamp with him? Scheherazade replied.

A young woman gave birth in the elevator of a hospital and felt very embarrassed about it.

To console her, one of the nurses said:
- You don't have to be embarrassed. Two years ago, a woman gave birth right in the maternity hospital courtyard.
Upon hearing this, the young mother burst into tears:
- I know, it was still me...

Two girls were discussing their recent adventures.

Last night, I spent 5 hours with a guy, one of them said disappointedly.
- Wow... cool. Why are you dissatisfied?
- Because for 3 hours he begged me, and for 2 hours he apologized!

The husband comes home in the evening, tired and angry.

The wife happily jumps into his arms:
- My dear, I'm pregnant!
- You too?

A sophisticated lady enters an elegant hat boutique.

- How may we assist you?
- I would like a big hat, with some romantic touch, maybe in blue or green, perhaps with flowers or stylized fruits...
- Specifically, what are you thinking of?
- Specifically, a round of sex. But a beautiful hat would be nice too...

The secretary to the boss:

– Am I being fired?
– No. Why do you ask?
– Well, why did you remove the couch from the office?

Taking advantage of the crowded bus, a guy persistently touches the woman in front of him.

She turns her head and says annoyed:
– Sir, please...
– There's no need to ask, I do it with pleasure...

Yesterday, I went to the forest and picked mushrooms for my mother-in-law.

– What if they are poisonous?
– What do you mean, "if"?

A student enters the girls' dormitory.

The security guard asks:
- Who are you visiting?
- Who do you advise me to visit?

Next to a condom vending machine, a message on the wall says:

"This is the worst chewing gum I've ever chewed!"

The little Indian asks his father, the great chief:

– Father, why do we, Indians, have such complicated names?

Son, it's due to a beautiful custom! We, Indians, are the only people who name their children after life events. For example, when your mother and I conceived your brother, one of the most beautiful falcons we had ever seen flew over our tent. That's why we named him Red Falcon. And when your sister was born, it was a clear night, hence the name Full Moon. As for you, you were unplanned. We didn't want any more children. Now you understand why we, Indians, are called likes this, Broken Rubber?

CLOSING THOUGHTS

Thank you so much for joining us on this journey of laughter and fun.

If you've had as much fun reading this book as we had writing it, then I consider our mission accomplished. Remember, laughter is the best medicine, and a day without a joke is a day wasted.

In the world of comedy, your feedback is gold. It helps authors tailor our content to the likes and dislikes of our readers. If this book brought a smile to your face, a laugh to your lips, or even lightened your day, then we would be honored if you would take a moment to leave a review.

Thank you for choosing 'Dirty Joke Book for Adults', and remember: keep laughing, because life is simply too short not to indulge in a good, dirty joke.

Until next time, keep those laughs coming!

lowebooks.com

Printed in Great Britain
by Amazon